Women Sharing Our Stories

Tompkins Park Senior Writers Association

Women Sharing Our Stories

Women Sharing Our Stories

Published 2023 by Tompkins Park Senior Writers Association
Tompkins Park Senior Writers Association
550 Greene Avenue Apt #7W
Brooklyn, NY 11216

First edition 2023 by Tompkins Park Senior Writers Association
Printed in the United States of America

Library of Congress Control Number: 2023913611
ISBN-13:   979-8-9873421-0-7 (Regular Print/Paperback)
             979-8-9873421-1-4 (eBook/Epub)
             978-0-9909558-1-8 (Large Print/Paperback)

Editors: Donna Williams, Bernice Elizabeth Green
Cover and Layout Design: Dree Morin, Dreemer Designs
                    www.dreemerdesigns.com

Contributing Artist: Darcella Jones
We thank Darcella for providing all drawings and artworks to accompany
our stories.

A Message to Our Readers

My reason for leading the class is my firm belief that we all have a story to share. I wanted to create the space for that to happen. For my class, it was stretching them to do things they had never done. For me, it was honoring the memory of my friend, Beverlee Bruce, and being committed to following through on my promise to her "to write our stories".

The journey has been long, but steady and I am thankful not only for Beverlee encouraging me, but also my class for accepting the challenge. Thank you: Bertha Brooks, Salina Coleman, Debra Johnson, Darcella Jones, Matilda Lloyd, Ruth Peters, Frances Sentino, Claudette Smith-Winston, Carole Stewart, and Terri Mardina Strobert for accepting the opportunity!! Finally a special shout out to Frances Sentino, who has been an ongoing member of the class since its inception in 2015!

— Selma Jackson
Creative Writing Instructor

Our Stories

MRS. BERTHA BROOKS

1933-2022

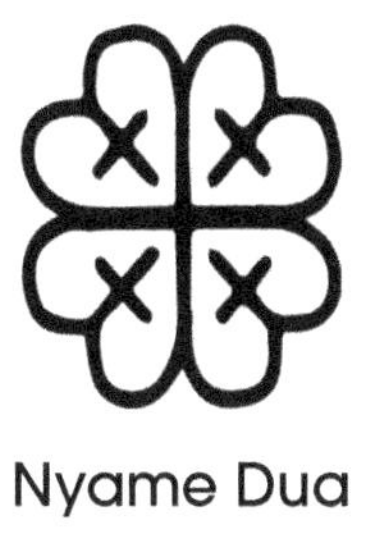

Nyame Dua

In Loving Memory

Mrs. Bertha Brooks, our eldest participant, lived on my floor at the Cornerstone Senior Housing complex. When I moved into the building, she welcomed me, and we became neighbors and friends. We were part of a breakfast club of four residents, and we celebrated our birthdays together!

I was so appreciative of Mrs. Bertha Brooks joining our writing class. While her declining memory did not allow her to write, she shared compelling stories during class about growing up in The South. We all listened intently, mesmerized, when she spoke.

To this day, we remember Mrs. Brooks fondly, and are grateful for her gift of total recall.

It is to her loving memory, this book is dedicated.

— Selma Jackson

From the first day I met Mrs. Brooks, I fell in love with her!

She was a gentle spirit, she possessed a godly presence, and showed sincere enthusiasm for her Tompkins Park Senior Center family.

She put so much joy into my heart, inspiring me by her presence and her warm memories of times past. I even thought of her as my own mentor and counselor. She shared great stories with our writing group, and I especially loved listening to her talk about her children.

Although saddened by her physical challenges that prohibited her from participating in more activities at the Center, I was honored that she did her best to attend as many of my wellness workshop sessions as she could.

During her life, I prayed every day for God to strengthen and heal her in mind, body, and spirit. But I know she is resting now.

I miss her so much, yet her motivating spirit is still alive here at the Center.

— Salina Coleman

My mother, Mazarina Johnson, and Mrs. Bertha Brooks were long-time friends at Cornerstone Senior Housing here in Brooklyn.

Mrs. Brooks' smile and sweet spirit always lifted me. I always looked forward to her story contributions to our workshop sessions.

I miss her and was blessed to have had a chance to meet and spend time with her during my stay in NY.

— Debra A. Johnson

Mrs. Brooks, you were lovely and kind.

Thank you for your legacy of love, your guidance, and your instructions on caring.

We learned so much from you through your interactions with your son; the bonds you created with each one of us as friend and sister; your warm stories, and regards for your history and roots.

Rest in Peace, Mrs. Brooks. Your work on Earth is ongoing, and continues to inspire.

— Frances Sentino

My condolences to the family of Mrs. Brooks and may she Rest in Peace.

The quiet one and soft-spoken lady in the class, Mrs. Brooks shared stories of being raised in The South and taught by Black teachers.

As a mother and wife, she loved and raised her children and led her family. As a woman, she took no stuff from anyone. God is smiling.

— Terri Strobert

Mrs. Bertha Brooks, who passed August 1, 2022, is seen here with her son in the dining room of the Tompkins Park Neighborhood Senior Citizens Center complex.
(Photo credit: Tompkins Park Senior Center)

RUTH PETERS

Ruth Peters was born in St. Vincent and the Grenadines. She moved to the United States in 1990 and settled in Brooklyn, where she still resides. Ruth's first job was as a domestic. After 10 years as a domestic, she became a home health aide for 17 years until her retirement. Now in retirement, Ruth enjoys programs at Tompkins Park Senior Center.

Dwennimmen

Island Girl, Humble Beginnings

I grew up in my native country of St. Vincent and the Grenadines. I am the second of seven children from my mother, three boys and four girls.

Growing up on the island was hard but we had a lot of food. My dad was a farmer, and he planted all kinds of provisions from fruits to vegetables. There were a lot of things we did not have, but it was not a problem. We were content.

In part, I had a rough life. I was very shy and reserved. I did not have many friends and I still do not, but I am wiser now. I choose my few friends wisely and they are very good friends. I am older, so I have learned to lighten up.

As a child, I helped my parents on the land and with my family. I had to get up early before school started. My chore was to go to the farm to get milk and bring it home so my mother could make the breakfast.

I would take breakfast to my dad at work, return home, then eat my breakfast and go to school. Every day, I had to run to get there because the teacher would be standing at the door waiting for all latecomers with the strap. There was no excuse for lateness.

At lunchtime, the routine started all over again. I would run up the hill to get home, take dad his lunch and start running back to school before the bell rang the second time. I learned to sprint, jump river stones and leap to get back to school in time.

I managed to make it to the fourth grade.

At age thirteen, I left school to help my mother with my brothers and sisters. When she became ill, my father would provide food for us but he eventually moved on with his life. I had to take responsibility for the home.

I found a job at 13 to help my mother in meeting the needs of the family. I didn't have to buy food, but my working provided for our other needs.

My mother was very loving, and she brought us up the best way that she knew how. When she was ten, her own mother died. My mom was a very good cook. During the week, our meals would be callaloo soup and pelau but on Sundays it was different. On the dinner table, we would have rice and peas, plantains, sweet potatoes, and dasheen as a side dish with stew beef or chicken. Brown stew fish was everyone's favorite meal! We drank lime juice or pineapple Kool-Aid, my favorite. And my dad would bring his friends for Sunday dinner.

In the evenings when there was a full moon, we kids would sit in the yard in the moonlight and eat a bowl of mangoes. There were all different sorts of mangoes, and we gave them names: Judy mangoes, Palowee, Palover, Debeek and Big Bitch. It was such a delightful time for the neighborhood kids. We were permitted to gather and eat as many mangoes as we wanted.

The older folks would share Anansi stories. In the dimness of the moonlight, these stories were scary and awesome at the same time.

"The Spider and the Fly"

"Will you walk into my parlor?" said the
  spider to the fly.

"This the prettiest little parlor that ever you
  may spy.

The way into my parlor is up a winding stair,
  and I have many curious things to show
  you when you're there."

"Oh no, no," said the little fly. "To ask me is
  in vain...

for who goes up your winding stair can never
  come down again."

"I'm sure you must be weary, dear, with
  soaring up so high.

Will you rest upon your little bed?" said the
  spider to the fly.

"There are pretty curtains drawn around; the
  sheets are fine and thin...

And if you like to rest a while, I'll snugly tuck
  you in!"

"Oh no, no," said the little fly, "for I've often
  heard it said...

'They never, never walk again who sleep upon
  your bed.'"

Said the cunning spider to the fly, "Dear
  friend, what can I do...

to provide the warm affection I've always felt
  for you?

I have within my pantry good stores of all
  that's nice.

I am sure you are welcome – will you please
  take a slice?"

"Oh no, no," said the little fly, "Kind sir, that
    cannot be:

I've heard what's in your pantry, and I do not
    wish to see!"

"Sweet creature," said the spider,

"You're witty and you're wise.

How handsome are your gauzy wings; how
    brilliant are your eyes!

I have a little looking glass upon my
    parlor shelf,

If you'd step in for one moment, dear, you
    shall behold yourself."

"I thank you, gentle sir," she said,

"For what you are pleased to say.

And bidding you good morning now, I'll call
    another day."

The spider turned him round about,
    and went into his den,

For well he knew the silly fly would soon
    come back again:

So he wove a subtle web in a little corner sly,
    and set his table ready to dine upon
    the fly;

Then came out to his door again
    and merrily did sing,

"Come hither, hither pretty fly,
    with pearl and silver wings.

Your robes are green and purples;
    there's a crest upon your head;

Your eyes are like diamonds bright,
    but mine are dull as lead!"

Alas, alas! How very soon this silly little fly,
    hearing his wily, flattering words, came
    slowly flitting by;

With buzzing wings she hung aloft,
    then near and nearer grew,
Thinking only of her brilliant eyes
    and green and purple hue.

Thinking only of her crested head,
    poor, foolish thing!
At last, up jumped the cunning spider,
    and fiercely held her fast;

He dragged her up his winding stair,
    into the dismal den.
Within his little parlor,
    but she never came out again!

And now, dear little children,
    who may this story read.
To idle, silly flattering words,
    I pray you never give heed;

Into an evil counselor close heart
    and ear and eye.
And take a lesson from this tale of
    the spider and the fly.

Ruth Peters

"How the Agouti Lost its Tail"

The animals were having a picnic, but they all
    had horns.
The dog didn't have horns, but he wanted to go.
So, he came up with a plan to make himself a pair
    of horns from cardboard.
When the time came for the picnic, the animals
    gathered on the pier to board the ship. The
    dog was there in disguise.
The Agouti was on the shore watching everyone
    on board.
Then suddenly called out, "Traitor on board.
    Traitor on board! Examine the horns!"
The animals did and found the dog with his false
    horns and threw him overboard.
So, the dog ran down the pier, chasing the Agouti.
As the Agouti entered into his hole, the dog bit
    off his tail.
And that's how the Agouti lost its tail.

Chief Joseph Chatoyer

Heroes who fought for freedom in the Caribbean are not well known in other cultures.

But school children in my native St. Vincent were taught our history.

We were told of the history of our national hero, Chief Joseph Chatoyer, at an early age. But who was he and what should we all know about his life.

Chatoyer, also known as Satuye, was a freedom fighter and leader of the indigenous population known as the Garifuna people, the Black Caribs.

Chatoyer revolted against slavery and oppression imposed by the British when they came to St. Vincent and the Grenadines. The two wars of what is known as the Carib Wars were from 1769-1773, and 1795-1797. Chatoyer was killed during battle on March 14, 1795.

Following his death, many Garifuna survivors were exiled by the British to the little islands called Balliceaux and Roatan, and into Central America in the countries of Belize, Guatemala, Honduras, and Nicaragua.

Chatoyer is celebrated and honored by all Garifuna descendants including those who live in the United States.

March 14th has been designated as a national holiday in St. Vincent and the Grenadines.

My written versions of the Anansi spider, one of the greatest characters in African folklore history are dedicated to my greatest achievements in life: my beloved children Patrick, Curtis, Rodney, and Camille; my eleven grandchildren; and one great grandchild; three brothers and three sisters; my other family members and friends. I credit the Tompkins Writers group for encouraging me to keep alive an important storytelling tradition of my heritage passed through the generations in the islands of St. Vincent and The Grenadines.

I never dreamed I would be a published author, a crowning achievement in my life.

MATILDA LLOYD

Matilda Lloyd describes herself as a proponent of the power of self-motivation and prayer-in-action as self-empowerment. After working as a nurse for nearly three decades at such distinguished medical institutions as Woodcrest Rehabilitation & Residential Health Care Center in Flushing, NY; Brooklyn Jewish Hospital & Medical Center (closed 1983); and Long Island Jewish Medical Center in New Hyde Park, NY, Ms. Lloyd made the decision to enroll in college to complete interrupted studies, while she was in her 50's. Against all odds, she persevered and obtained a double master's degree in early Childhood Education and in Special Education. But her greatest joys are entrenched in "serving the Lord by ministering to whoever needs to hear the Word of Life;" being the mother of three biological children, including one who passed in childbirth; and fostering a host of other young people over the years into adulthood.

Ode Nyera Fie Kwan

My Life's Challenges: More than Enough

(Bible Scripture References: King James Version)

One cannot move through life without a challenge on one level or another. Some are small and easy to overcome; others large and formidable. I have had my share of provocations, obstacles, hurdles, difficulties, and problems. I have managed some and juggled others.

In this three-section passage I focus on two events that occurred in – and still shape – my life; with the third section, written in the form of a dramatic monologue, presenting the point of view of an elder, who at first is challenged by and then challenges the younger generation to heed an ancestral calling.

For all stories, prayer is seen as more than enough to navigate the impass-able, and to overcome tests to the body, soul and the spirit.

Part I: Personal Journey

Besides the routine challenges we must face in life from the moment of our conception to the moment of our last breath, some of us are burdened with impossible and most difficult challenges along our journey.

For me, a steadfast believer in the Word of God, I rely on my Faith to overcome each challenge faced. It is my anchor every step of the way: before, during, and after every trial and tribulation that has attempted to knock me out of the game of life.

In fact, one of my greatest testimonies is about a challenging experience of March 31, 2008, which tests me to this day.

Upon leaving my apartment heading to church, I turned to lock my door. I could not afford to waste any time because I needed to get to church before my Sunday School students arrived. Suddenly, my head felt funny. I stood still for a few seconds to let the feeling pass.

I waited on Nostrand Avenue for the bus for about 15 minutes. When it didn't come, I walked up to Fulton St. and still there was no bus. I hailed a cab. I arrived at church just a few minutes before my first student.

It was a busy Sunday for me. After teaching Sunday School class, as the Christmas Club Collection Fund secretary, I was called in to action. I was one of the table secretaries for the Expense Offering; and one of the secretaries that had to verify the correct amount of each offering received that day. By that time, I was extremely exhausted, but my word is my bond. I did as I had promised I would do.

At the close of the morning service, my niece asked, "Are you staying for evening service?" I told her I would go home to rest.

Later, just before midnight, my niece called to check up on me just as I was going to the bathroom. I let her know that I had fallen three times before getting there. She asked me if I wanted her to drive from Westchester County to Brooklyn to get me to the hospital. I declined, thinking I would just go back to bed.

On the way back to bed, the Spirit of God spoke to me clearly and concisely, "If you lay back down again, you won't get back up."

I called my niece and told her I would take a bath and hail a cab downstairs on Nostrand Ave. I did not want to inconvenience her because she lived in Mount Vernon and she had to teach the next day in the Bronx, NY. Within a few minutes, I was on the phone calling her back. My mind was foggy but I managed to tell her with an urgency: "Come and get me."

When we arrived at Kings County Hospital, she let me out at the Emergency Room Doors so that she could find parking. At the Triage desk, the nurse, overwhelmed with paperwork, did not even look up. She asked, "How may I help you?"

I heard myself saying, "I think I'm having a stroke." She looked up from her paperwork, and said, "Smile!" Then she told me to lift both hands together. Everything after that was a blur. She did not ask for my name, rank, or serial number. Or insurance card.

For the rest of the night, I took a series of tests, scans, X-rays, MRIs and Brain Tests, one after the other.

I was admitted to the Urgent Critical Care Unit, and woke up in a very large room enclosed all around by windows. That room was right beside the Nurses Station so that I could be monitored and it was full of emergency Life Support-equipment. I tried to get up, I could not move. I became hysterical and started crying, "What in the world did I do that I am tied down like this!? What did I do!?"

I knew, as a matter of fact, that I must have done something dangerous to be strapped down to a hospital bed. The nurse asked me, "What's wrong?" I replied with a question, "Why am I tied down, what did I do!?"

The nurse responded, "Stop that, you know what God can do!" I recalled a scripture: Philippians 4:13 says, *I can do all things through Christ which strengtheneth me.*

I repeated, "But, why am I tied down!" Then it hit me like a ton of bricks. I said, horrified, "I'm paralyzed!?" I was flabbergasted, just could not believe it. She said again emphatically, "Stop It, You Know What God Can Do!"

Then she asked, "Why are you trying to get up?" I said, "I need to go to the bathroom." She said, "You have a catheter inserted." Then in a very soothing quiet and encouraging voice, she said, "You know what God can do," and left the room.

I knew for certain that I had suffered a stroke. I was in Kings County Hospital for six weeks and I never saw that nurse again. I still wonder if that encounter with that nurse was an actual event or a visitation from one of God's angels that had been sent to let me know God's plan was at work in my life.

Jeremiah 29:11 says, *For I know the thoughts that I think toward you, saith the Lord, thoughts of peace, and not of evil, to give an expected end.*

Her words never left my mind since that day. When that nurse left the room, I remember praying, "Lord, I think I know what that Scripture means. I've heard it preached so many, many times. I've even given a discourse on it a few times. So, what then are you saying to me exactly, when you say, 'You know what God can do.'"

The Lord answered me, "My Grace is sufficient." 2 Corinthians 12:9 says, *And he said unto me, My grace is sufficient for thee: for my strength is made perfect in weakness. Most gladly therefore will I rather glory in my infirmities, that the power of Christ may rest upon me.*

I prayed, "Lord, I am paralyzed (as if He did not know it). No one has ever helped me. I have always been the one who had to help others. How is your grace going to help me, now? In my spirit, I heard Him answer simply, "I'm more than enough!"

As I mentioned before, I was in Kings County Hospital for six weeks and at the Concord Rehabilitation Center for six weeks. At Kings County Hospital, I had to relearn how to perform several of life's basic functions all over again: speaking, bathing, dressing and feeding myself. I would miss my mouth and feed my bed often. I also had to lean how to walk again.

My six weeks of recovery at Kings County comprised a program to rebuild my mind, body, spirit, and soul. It continued with therapeutic regimens for Speech, Occupational, Dietary and Physical – the roughest and most frustrating of them all.

For Physical Therapy, I had two different routines on the parallel bars. First, I had to regain my general balance, then balance while standing before I could even attempt to walk.

At rehab, I continued the therapeutic regimens: Physical, Speech, Occupational, and Dietary Therapy. The most frustrating of these routines continued to be Physical Therapy. The first exercises at the Rehab were a continuation of the work on the parallel bars. During this task, as before at Kings County Hospital, I was strapped in between two parallel bars and was instructed to grab hold of a toy animal with my left hand. That was torturous; as soon as I was about to grab the toy, it was snatched away. This continued for about ten or more times. I got so angry that I cried out, "Why do you keep doing this?" I later realized the purpose was to retrain my general balancing skills.

I had to learn to crawl and take "baby steps" again which would enable me to stand before I could attempt to walk. I had a heavy firm strap fastened around my waist with a handle for the therapist to hold and control my movements. This process was very tedious because I had to confront and control my fear of falling.

Afterwards, I had to learn how to walk between the two parallel bars one step at a time without dragging my right foot.

The next therapeutic exercise was learning to walk with a walker-like contraption. Then on to learning to walk without assistance with the therapist close at hand instructing me first on how to take each step; how to position my body before taking each step; and how to always look up and straight ahead.

When I was discharged from rehab, I went back to my old walk-up apartment on Nostrand Ave. However, my entire medical team (doctors, nursing department, social workers, and therapists, along with my entire family) did not want me to return to that building with its many adverse detrimental medical strikes against it.

For me, the few positive features outweighed the negatives. Even though it did not have such a pleasant appearance to the eye, I believed it could be dressed and polished up over time.

In New York City, storage space is a premium. I loved, loved, loved this apartment because it had a huge premium walk-in room size closet, a nice size coat closet, an exceptional size pantry, and many other smaller sized storage spaces.

This apartment was situated right next to the Nostrand Ave bus stop. Within several short blocks in either direction (north, south, east, or west), there were at least ten bus routes. Right across the street there was a laundromat.

And finally, there were only two other tenants besides me living in the building, and eventually we always looked out for each other.

The rehab process continued back home. I had to relearn, alone, the daily routines of living by myself with several critical disabilities: the lack of use of my paralyzed dominant right hand; the loss of functioning in my right leg; and performing physical and mental tasks with only half a brain.

It was made known to me by my doctors that when a brain stroke occurs on one side of the brain the opposite side of the body can be paralyzed.

There were two flights of stairs that I had to climb to reach my second-floor apartment. Because of my disability and the fact that there was one stair railing along one hallway wall, I had to be extremely cautious going down the steps rather than ascending them. I was very fearful of falling. So, as I slowly took each cautious step, I prayed constantly and held my breath. After the last step, I would hold the doorknob for a few minutes and breathe deeply and freely.

Learning to cook again was among the hardest activities I had to endure because of the daily chores. That was because I never really liked to cook in the first place. Having only one hand to work with made it a grueling process. It still is now. Yet, I did my own laundry, cleaning, shopping, and bathing. Just slower.

You may be wondering, how in the world did she do all that with her non-dominant left hand? Well, it was not of my own strength or power. When I woke up paralyzed from the stroke, I remembered Philippians 4:13, *I can do all things through Christ which strengtheneth me.*

I had a choice: I could stand up to these challenges life threw my way, or I could give in and throw in the towel. There was no choice; I never gave up, and I never gave in to the late-night "Pity Parties" or "Poor-Me" whining.

When I confronted a challenging dilemma, I stopped and prayed, Lord Jesus, show me how to get it done with only one hand. Immediately, it was as though a dark cloud had just rolled away, and I could instantly see a solution to my problem.

Regarding my housing dilemma, before I could have any say in the matter, my hospital's medical team, my family, and my church's clergy team had arranged for me to move into a senior citizen's elevated apartment building. Then came my Big Girl Challenge: The Move.

Hate is a very strong word; however, I hated the very thought of moving: the packing; the decisions on what to take with me, what to throw away, and what to give away.

And then there were the appliances and other things I was told I could not bring with me to the new apartment.

I had two appliances that were practically brand new: a washing machine and a refrigerator which I still fret about every time I leave my current apartment to go down to the laundromat and or when my refrigerator acts up.

My children live in upstate New York, so I had to do all the packing myself. They came on moving day and got the U-HAUL packed and unpacked.

I really had to depend on God's help with this challenge. When something was too high for me to reach, I would ask God how I could climb up to reach it. There was no answer at all, just dead silence. The stupid question did not deserve an answer.

When my family came with the U-Haul, they got those things down that were up too high for me to safely reach. The last part of this process that I had to do by myself was the unpacking of boxes, organizing things before storing them away, and finally the gathering of the trash and boxes for the garbage.

It took me about six to eight months or so to make the new home livable. Thanks to God, I got it all done with only that one good hand, the one good leg, and half a functioning brain.

That brain stroke happened a little more than 15 years ago. Yet, "still I rise." In the spirit of Maya Angelou who rose through all her challenges, I, too, have prevailed through dilemmas.

Lord Jesus, show me how to get it done with only one hand, I would pray. Immediately, it was as if a dark cloud had just rolled away, and I could instantly see the answer to my problem. After a while, I determined the answer was inside me already. Psalms 118:17 says, *I shall not die, but live, and declare the works of the Lord.*

All of life's challenges have a purpose and a goal from the moment of our conception until the moment of death. I believe our collective goal should be to determine the moral significance and practical lessons obtained from our challenging experiences.

A few questions we should ask ourselves along the journey are: What did I learn from the experience? How did it make me a better human being? Did my thinking skills improve? Did my experience enhance my behavior skills, including character, morale, treatment of my fellow human beings? And so on.

The life lessons gained from my personal challenges have been many. Yet, the solution to all of them are anchored in Philippians 4:11: *Not that I speak in respect of want: for I have learned, in whatsoever state I am, therewith to be content.*

I do not complain about my limp right arm with its paralyzed right hand; or my non-functioning right leg attached to my right foot I drag along the floor when I am not wheel-chair bound; or my half-brain.

Every day I wake up, I am whole. I have another day to be grateful to be alive.

Part II: My Childhood Family Challenge

My mother was, in essence, a single mother even though she was married to my father.

My father was called a Jack-of-All-Trades. He worked day and night, wherever he could find work, to provide for his family.

Most of the time, he was away from home. When he did come home, he would use whatever money he had made to pay something on the bills.

His most profitable job was as a garbage man. In the white neighborhoods, he cleared out their junk and collected whatever was no longer of any value to them anymore. He would repair these items and bring them home to us. The rest he sold to the Blacks in our neighborhoods.

My grandfather had taken my mother out of the third grade to take care of her 20+ siblings after my grandmother died in childbirth.

When my mother got old enough, she married her first husband. They had three children together. Later, he divorced her, and my mother married again – to my father.

I was the sixth child of nine siblings. The three oldest children had grown up and left home. After they left home, I was the oldest girl of those still at home and became responsible for my brothers and sister still at home.

We all had chores.

There was no such thing as girl jobs or boy jobs. These chores were interchangeable. We did whatever my mother assigned us to do. She would have the boys do what was thought of as women's work. These jobs included things like washing dishes, washing clothes, cooking, ironing, cleaning the house, and even babysitting the three youngest children. While I, as the oldest girl, did what was generally thought of as men's work. I had to chop wood for the fire; haul coal home from the store; and collect coal from the railroad tracks that had fallen from the freight trains behind our house.

At night, it was my responsibility to bring in the coal and wood for the fire I had to make the next morning. If I had forgotten to bring those in at night, I would have to find a way to dry them out before I could make a fire. We didn't have running water inside the house, nor a flushing toilet. Both were outside. Therefore, water had to be brought inside every morning for daily use.

Every morning we had to clean the house, clean again after school, and a final cleaning before going to bed at night. There was always something to do. My mother had a mastery of proverbs and old adages. She said that idle hands were the devil's workshop. She kept us busy.

My mother was a strict disciplinarian. There was no talking back; no questioning her orders; no disputing an older adult, and the list goes on and on. All adults in the neighborhood were your extended parents.

If they believed you were misbehaving, they could use the rod of correction, and if they told your parents, you got the rod of correction again.

We seldom got to go outside to play and then for only a little while. It wasn't long before she found another chore for us to do. One of us had to sweep and scrub the porch with a broom. Another one of us had to sweep and clean the dirt yard until it looked like it was polished.

I really enjoyed church, and I enjoyed school also. These were mostly the only times we children got out of the house on a regular basis. Sometimes we went to the market with her to help bring the groceries home.

My mother was a strict disciplinarian. If her directions weren't understood, she would simply say, "Get it done."

I would classify my mother and my relationship as a love/hate one. But after her demise, I realized that I loved her, but was never able to tell her while she was alive.

She needed to hear it; I needed to say it, and vice versa. If she can appreciate this salute from beyond, I give it with a grateful heart.

Mama, I wish I had told you how much I loved you before you fell asleep in that permanent rest.

I would classify our relationship as an oxymoron, a love/hate, relationship.

A love/hate relationship because I couldn't for the life of me understand why you were so much harder on me than any of my other siblings. You made me "responsible" for them obeying your strict rules and regulations.

Yet, you did not give me any authoritative power to enforce those orders. Nevertheless, I got punished for their misbehavior. I wasn't allowed to question your rules. So, when I got punished with the rod of correction and my face showed my displeasure, you would come up behind me and give me a backhanded slap in my mouth. That was worse than a thousand lashes because it made me feel humiliated and worthless.

I never could have expressed myself like this while you were alive. I hated those slaps in the mouth, but I loved and respected you so much more and I never ever wanted to hurt your feelings.

Mama, it's only since I've had the responsibilities of raising my own children that I understood how difficult it was for you.

Mama, it's only now since I'm an old great-grandma that I wish I had told you how much I appreciated your discipline, correction, and directions.

Mama, you mastered the art of being a strict disciplinarian. I continue to live by your rules of conduct.

I can still hear you and see you giving me that sideways look that says, "Shut up!" Your discipline, your corrections, and your directions still work in my life.

To this very day I will not even consider doing certain things; I fear you will show up.

The "Prison System Challenge" or Listen, My Children!
(Message to Our Young People presented as a Monologue)

Listen, my children and hear some words of sound wisdom from an old snot like me! One who's insignificant to you! Not worth paying any attention to, at all.

Where shall I begin? Well, let's define insignificant.

My children, don't you look at each other with smirks on your faces! I am ... Yo' Mama!! Yo' Grandma!! Yo' Great Grandma!!

And you know what big words like that mean.

So, let me attempt, again, to give y'all a meaningful message.

Children, let's start with words. Like in-sig-ni-fi-cant. Webster's Dictionary defines it in many ways. But the one that hit home is the one you understand: Not Even Worth Considering AKA Very Unimportant.

Y'all expresses y'all contempt in all kinds a ways – verbal, body (especially when yuh tense up), facial expressions. Y'all reveal y'all true intentions every which way and it all winds up to mean "You are of little or no meaningful value to us at all. You very unimportant and you not even worth the time of day to listen to."

John 8:32 reveals that *you shall know the truth, and that truth will set you free.* Y'all may say, "What does that have to do with anything?"

Well, it has significant meaning. You do agree that Truth or what's real is significant, right?

Well, I'm significant to God, even if I'm not significant to you. I'm important to God, even if I'm not important to you, and your lives matter to God even if you don't matter to you; I have value to God, even if you don't find value in me!

Listen, children, there are certain things that y'all don't realize. I cherished every kick in my womb. I smiled through the tears at when y'all first cry when y'all were born. I loved it when I could get y'all to sleep throughout the night.

I enjoyed y'all terrible stages: when y'all had those temper tantrums, I would get down on the floor and have them with you, except I was louder and crazier than y'all were. Then y'all would stop mid-cry with the wildest expression on y'all face like: "Are you crazy, woman!"

Those were the best and most satisfying times because they produced the best results possible: no more temper tantrums.

On our daily walks to school when I helped y'all practice for y'all weekly spelling and math tests. Then on the day of the tests, saying to y'all, now bring me home an A+. I had high expectations and high hopes for y'all.

It meant I believed in your significance.

Now, what can be said about those horrible teenage years when there was a crisis behind everything. I wonder now, how did either of us make it through those dilemmas.

Then it became time for Law and Order, when I lay down the laws of "my house" – with my pursed lips, my big eyes my head shaking – I stood my ground and declared, "as long as you live in my house, you gonna obey my rules!"

Listen children, let's get back to John 8:32. That was the truth y'all should have learned back then; and if y'all had obeyed the truth back then, y'all truth would have set y'all free from the "Harsh Disciplines" and apart from the "prison system".

Y'all thought I was so harsh and mean, but those rules weren't so easy for me to enforce either. Nevertheless, I was under the directives of the highest government authority, the Master of the Universe, my Almighty God. I had a direct order from God Himself. In Proverbs 22:6, He ordered me to "Raise" you "in the way you should go" so that when you're fully grown and matured "you will abide by the word."

I am a witness and a testimony to that principle even to this very day! When I was about to respond in a way that was against my mother's teachings and God's authority, I saw behind my eyelids, my mother's wide popping glaring eyes and her tightly sealed lips. She was saying, "Oh no, you don't"!

So, why would I say that? It's because I loved, honored, respected, and appreciated my mama as my mother.

And I loved her until the day God called her to her final resting place. Yes! I have regrets in my relationship with my mother!

I thought, she was hard on me. But I never disrespected her. If only (two of the saddest words in our English dictionary), I had told her how much I loved her before it was too late.

So, listen children, let's pull back the lens of life's camera. And zoom on you.

Do you remember how y'all constantly yearned for the day y'all could leave the home you called "Prison" and be out on y'all own and do whatever y'all wanted to do without having to answer to anybody?

Well, children, now y'all there! Not as great as you thought it would be, is it? Nothing like y'all imagined it to be, right?

I laughed on the inside when y'all loudly complained and y'all declared, 'I'm not going to make my children obey a lot of stupid rules and regulations'.

'I'm never gon' punish them for disobeying the rules.

'As a matter of fact, I'm not having any rules in my house at all. They won't need to have any chores to do, like makin' beds; cleaning rooms; washin' dishes; sortin' and washin' clothes. They won't have to do homework during summer vacation. My children will love me because I'm going to be they best friend!'"

Well, my children, now that your children are all grown up, Dr. Phil would say, "How is it working out for you?"

Seems to me they don't have any respect for you at all! They curse you out, they order you around like you're their puppet, and they expect you to obey them rather than the other way around.

So, children, let's look into camera lens again. But this time we're going to look forward. You're old and disabled: maybe physically, mentally, emotionally, psychologically, or terminally ill. Not able to help yourself at all.

Are your children your best friends, now?

Will they give you the time of day or will they admit you to a nursing home and never look or come back to see how you are, leaving you to die all alone? That's what you would call, children, a "Generational Curse."

Remember that this old snot tried to tell y'all that whatever y'all do will come back to y'all as a blessing or as a curse that will haunt y'all throughout the rest of your life?

Galatians 6:7 says, "Whatever you do will return to you in like manner." That means, do good and y'all will receive good; do evil and y'all will receive evil.

It's not too late to make a difference. If there's life, there's hope.

Parenting doesn't stop when you turn twenty-one; it continues throughout your life span. Your mother, grandmothers and great grandmothers are/were praying for each one of you.

They are trying to show you the right way and how to demonstrate good words through good actions – the right way.

When we are long gone, the teachings – if you listen to them and respect them – will always be with you, and carry you and your offspring and your generations down the long roads.

And that's significant.

FRANCES SENTINO

Frances Sentino is a retired Montessori teacher and a member of the Tompkins Park Writers Association. As a child, she often got in trouble for reading in the dark past her bedtime! Her love for reading turned into a passion for writing, which she continues to do to this day.

Frances' interests include baking, sewing, gardening, and traveling. She also enjoys spending time with her family, especially her two adult daughters and granddaughter. Frances lives in Brooklyn, NY, with her sister Florence, and her two cockatiels, Joy and Joe.

Visit her online at floressentino.com.

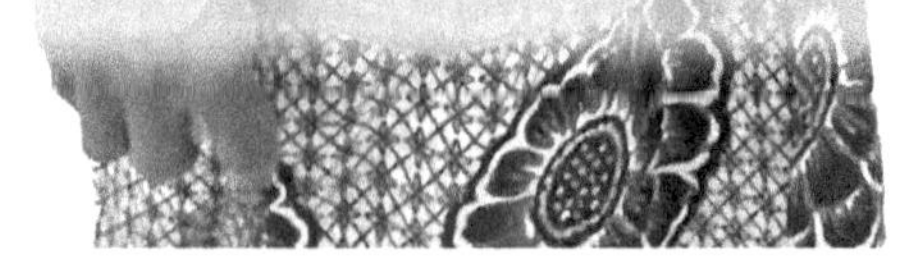

Sankofa

Finding My People

After several years believing my family's history was lost, my sister Joan Flores met our lost but not forgotten oldest senior family member elder, Cipriano Flores, Sr., my late father's uncle. Joan found my grand-uncle after many of her trips to America from Belize, 50 years ago.

Her life-changing encounter with our elder was a Godsend as Cipriano, who was in his 80's, had left Belize C.A., decades earlier, after his mother died in childbirth. Even his immediate family had no contact with him.

My family belongs to the Garinagu *(plural of Garifuna)*, formally known as the Carib Indians of St. Vincent in the Caribbean. We are proud of our African and Indian roots and beliefs. At the core of our faith is a respect for our ancestors and their insights and traditions. So, when Cipriano left Belize, an important link in our extraordinary history travelled with him.

My people's history goes back hundreds of years on the island, long before the Europeans arrived in what they called "the new world", and they would die before becoming enslaved in the land they owned.

Between 1635-1675 slave ships bound for America sank or were shipwrecked near St. Vincent. Carib natives, led by the last chief Joseph Chatoyer, freed chained Africans and hid others who had escaped from the slave ships and swam ashore.

When war broke out between the French and the British, the British won. Many of the islands were colonized. Chief Chatoyer was killed. His followers were deported on smaller ships; many died at sea. Those who survived landed on an island near Honduras. I am descended from those brave people, who never forgot their roots.

Later, some natives departed Honduras seeking a home along the coast. They landed on Dandriga, the southern part of Belize. The Governor gave them permission to settle in that village and in Punto Gorda and other smaller areas.

Years later, my great-grandfather Flores travelled from Honduras to Dandriga, and met and married his wife, Luisa Roches de Flores.

They had three boys: Cipriano, Telesfore (my grandfather), and Victoriano. When their mother died during child-birth, an aunt raised two of the brothers, Telesfore and Victoriano. When he was old enough Victoriano followed his dad to Honduras. Cipriano remained in Dangriga and worked with Jesuit priests who knew his parents. Later, Cipriano journeyed to the United States and lost contact with his family.

Through a cousin, Thomas Joseph, who joined the Divine Word Missionaries in Bay St. Louis, Mississippi, my father learned that his Uncle Cipriano was alive, married and living in Mobile, Alabama. Dad and my paternal grand-uncle, Cipriano, then in his 80's, exchanged family photos and kept in touch.

If everyone found their families, what stories, great stories we could share. If we do not know, we would disappear. To know means you have something to live for and to fight for. It makes you sharp and strong.

My heritage is a story of people who fought slavery and the harshest elements of capitalism and colonialism. They also never forgot where they came from.

Thus, I am blessed by the research of my sister, and the knowledge that my visionary ancestors repeated their stories down the line for many years so that we could share them with others.

My Parents Taught Me to Pray

I thank God every day that my parents taught me how to place my burdens in the hand of the Lord or at the foot of His Cross.

To tell you the truth I do not know how I would have faced all my troubles, if I had not known the power of prayer and God's goodness and love for his people, at an early age.

In my village many people died after Hurricane Hattie, surviving it taught me to lean on God with prayers.

My parents had seven children, my dad worked as a teacher, and my mom stayed home with us. There was always cooked food and baked bread on our table.

Even though there was only one salary, my parents were able to pay for our high school education. We continued our education from there.

My sister, Joan, the first to graduate from high school, went directly to the convent; she celebrated sixty years there in June 2019.

Louise, Florence and I became teachers; Julia, a homemaker like our mom; Christina, a registered nurse, and our brother Matthew, an official with the Agricultural Department of the Belize government.

Mom and dad encouraged us to work hard, but most of all, we were taught to have God first in our lives. It is important that we do the same for our children and grandchildren, especially now; young people today have so much more to deal with than we did when we were their ages.

So, what is prayer? It is speaking to God. Prayer teaches discipline and focus. It inspires good habits. We had night prayer at home, every night. We memorized entire Bible passages.

We were strong during troubling times.

The well-known devastating Hurricane Hattie, ripped through Belize on October 31, 1961, wrecking our Mullins River village, and leveling everything in its path moving along the Caribbean Sea coast, north of Dandriga.

It flooded homes and ruined lives; work needed to be done. Prayer gave us power. Led by our father, we did the work ourselves. We rebuilt the house on stilts. Just like our ancestors did.

Why I Write

I write because I have something to say, and much to share.

With so much going on in our daily lives, from moment to moment, it is difficult for me *not* to take pen to paper.

Most of the time, I confess I write to have something to refer to when I need the information later or when I think someone else will benefit from useful information.

I write more these days about how I feel, positive or negative; what I see; and the people I meet.

When I am happy, I find myself writing about it.

When I am sad, writing down my many Blessings fills me with such joy and transforms my mood and outlook about given situations.

Writing connects me to my feelings and thoughts at any given time and in any given situation. One of the things I am thinking and feeling about writing is that it is connecting me to a higher purpose while I am here on earth.

It is an indelible link to those who will come after us. It gives them a record of events. It offers the tools to use to survive.

Writing is evidence to leave behind for our loved ones to understand more about us and the world. It is a way to tell our stories in our words. It is a record for life itself.

CLAUDETTE SMITH-WINSTON

Claudette was born in and lived most of her 80 years in the 11216 zip code of the Bedford-Stuyvesant section of Brooklyn, New York. She was educated in the public school system and graduated in 1960 from Wingate High School. The next eight years she worked for the New York City Welfare Department. She married in 1963 and left New York to reside in New Jersey for the next ten years. When she returned to New York in 1973 with her two children, she worked as office manager at the Clinton Auto School until her retirement.

Ankh

My Hair, My Trauma

I believe I was born with a head full of hair, but what went wrong? I don't know. All I know is, all my life I have had some trauma or issue with my hair or about my hair.

In my early childhood years, somebody was always trying to do something to my head of "bad" – you know: nappy, unruly, unmanageable very short on each side and in the back – hair. So that meant I never had enough hair to make a ponytail, something I desired all my childhood.

Adding to my misery, my mother gave birth to my brother two years after me, and guess what? He had a head full of curly hair which grew so long my mother had to braid it. When he went to the barber for his first haircut, my mother clipped and saved one of his long curly locks.

My family all tried to help me with my hair issues. They did everything to make me look like a girl, but my hair would not grow. Even Gramma, my great grandmother, would sit me on the floor, between her legs and tie string or thread around a million little braids she made on my head. This was supposed to help my hair grow. Not only did it fail to make my hair grow, but it hurt like HELL and got no positive results from her effort.

My mother tried her best to deal with my hair before she turned me over to my father's sister; Aunt Bea did a better job managing my hair issues because she had short hair herself and she knew what to do with my hair.

I remember – my second-grade teacher, Ms. Rosen, made me somewhat self-conscious about my hair, or lack of it. There were two girls in my class – Beverly and Carol – who were light, bright and had hair down their backs.

I wondered why these two girls were the "teacher's pets". Ms. Rosen never called on me to be a monitor, erase the blackboard, or do any of the things a favored student did. Well, thank God, I got through those early childhood hair trauma days.

As I get older, I remember – My Great-Aunt Carrie! She did hair in her home and was given the task of "doing" my hair. Aunt Carrie straightened every hair on my head including the little hairs that grew on the base of my head and my neck (they called that area, The Kitchen!). She also straightened all the short edges around my head. My head was on fire when she finished. I didn't enjoy these encounters to say the least.

When Aunt Carrie retired, my mother sent me to the beauty parlor every two weeks. This trend continued through adulthood. I then discovered perms and relaxers. They kept me out of the beauty parlor every two weeks. I tried wigs but I never liked, nor loved wearing them. I did my own hair and I was pleased with my hair. For a while.

When the Afro became the style for Black people, I was scared to cut the perms out of my hair to start my Afro, so I let my Afro grow in naturally. I wore it for many years.

I remember – one day I was complaining about my 'fro. It was beginning to look crazy. My hair would not grow evenly on all sides of my head. My brother-in-law heard me and said if I leave my hair alone it would grow. He suggested I try the locs. I didn't believe him. I fussed and cussed about my unruly Afro. Finally, I let my sister loc my hair at the ripe old age of 50 plus. I left my hair alone and it grew and grew. And grew. The first thing I did when my hair reached my shoulders on all sides was to go to my room alone and put my hair in a ponytail for the first time in my life. I was happy as a pig in mud! For that moment.

I was able to maintain my locs myself with little or no care for the next few years. But I believe locs have a mind of their own – at least mine did, especially as they aged. It cost a fortune to keep them pruned and groomed.

Now, my hair has returned to its childhood state, unruly, out of control, unmanageable, no growth on the sides, etc.

What can I do; my hair has come full circle.

My Heroes and Sheroes

My #1 Shero and Hero: My Mom, the Homemaker, and my Dad, the Breadwinner. Their roles never changed, and my mother never worked.

My parents married young, ages 19 and 23, respectively. They had the responsibility of raising 8 children plus their first grandchildren. My mother also helped me raise my two children. Mom and Dad worked very hard fulfilling the needs of our large family. We had the best Christmases, Thanksgivings, picnics, backyard barbecues, plus car rides in the fall to see the changing of the seasons.

My dad passed at 57, but my mother was able to keep our household together because of my father's excellent work history. She also fulfilled her lifelong dream of going to college. At age 70, she received her B.A. degree from the College of New Rochelle.

My #2 Shero: My Paternal Aunt Bea, My Mentor. My love of sewing, music, crocheting, knitting, etc. came from my Aunt Bea. She always had a listening ear and lots of patience with me, especially when I was a teenager and my mom and I did not see eye-to-eye on things.

Aunt Bea was always there for me. We wound up working in the same field. She was an office manager for a chemical company, and I was an office manager at a driving school.

Aunt Bea was adventurous, and she loved the theater. She planned great trips all over the country and she always invited me along.

My #3 Hero: My 8th grade teacher, Mr. Haliburton. He was my first Black male teacher, such an inspiration to me. He was smart, wise, and a gentleman who saw more in me than I saw in myself. I got good grades in his class. He made it possible for me to be in his 9th grade graduating class, too. I was elated.

My #4 Shero: Aunt Carrie, my great aunt. She was the one who made it possible for our southern relatives to come North to start a new life. She either had a large apartment, a rented house, or her own home to achieve this goal. Aunt Carrie helped my grandparents bring my mother and two siblings to New York from North Carolina. Everybody stayed with Aunt Carrie until they were able to move out on their own. She worked hard, loved her family, friends, and her church. She never had children but loved us like we were her own. She took us many places, on bus rides, and put us in church programs.

Aunt Carrie gave big family dinners, plus she opened her heart and her home to all. She was always president of all the clubs and organizations she belonged to, and people always trusted her with their money. She did so much with the little bit of education she had. Amazing!

My #5 Hero: My boss for over 20 years, Mr. Williams. As noted, I was the office manager at his driving school. He encouraged me to learn how to drive which made it possible for me to get my first car. He also insisted that I take the Notary Public test. I passed the test, and I am still a Notary Public today. Mr. Williams brought in a computer instructor who taught me, one on one, most of the computer knowledge I have today. Mr. Williams was kind, patient, and always respectful of my right to be a good single parent to my children. I was able to earn extra money with my notary, computer, and driving skills. As a result, I was able to do a lot of things with my children, like our vacation to Disney World in Florida.

All my Heroes and Sheroes are gone now, but I learned so much from them.

SALINA COLEMAN

Salina G. Coleman was born and raised in Bedford-Stuyvesant, Brooklyn. Her early ambitions centered around making a difference in the lives of school-aged children. She enrolled in Boricua College with the intentions of obtaining a bachelor's degree in elementary education. As she entered her third year of studies in 1996, she was diagnosed with Systemic Lupus Erythematosus, and she has been living with its adverse effects for 25+ years. Even though her physical health can get severe at any given time, the former athlete says her "faith, will and spirit" refuse to allow the condition to hinder her from doing what she loves to do: developing, organizing and hosting wellness advocacy workshops for families, groups and individuals; speaking out on the personal impact of Lupus and other life-altering diseases; and strategically utilizing her personal gifts, which include Arts & Crafts, to deliver her messages.

Nsoroma

Exploring the Life of a Lupie
(A Survivor for Over 25 Years!)

I wish you could live inside my body for just one day, to get a sense of, and truly understand, the continual roller coaster ride I go through daily. We all have our ups and downs, but this ride – living with Lupus – is totally different for me.

I was diagnosed in 1996. This chronic illness, ever since, has been a living nightmare, turning my life upside down. The truth is Lupus impacts every part of a survivor's life – whether the effects can be seen or not. But there are parts of it, in my case, that are not visible.

So, what don't you see when you look at me?

You don't see...

- the pain migrating throughout my body at any given time of the day.
- when my limbs swell, ache, and throb...leaving me unable to use them any further.
- my hands hurting so badly that at times I cannot touch anything!
- the constant insomnia.
- the headache that pounds my head like a drum whenever it feels like it.
- the jaw pain that hinders me from eating.
- the mouth ulcers that agitate me whenever I swallow.

- the nose ulcers that pain my nostrils whenever I must blow my nose.
- the butterfly rash on my face or other rashes that suddenly flare up on my body!
- the 20+ plus pills I must take, and the work setting up and keeping track of the schedule.
- how my body gets cold all the time and what I must do to keep warm using various alternative methods, including heating pads, multiple blankets and even my blow dryer.
- how my desires have changed because of chronic fatigue, and I tend not to engage in or do most of the things I love to do and use to do.
- the frequent visits to not one, but multiple doctors and countless laboratory tests.
- the constant mood swings between feeling happy and content to feeling the heaviest burden of sadness, anxiety, and frustration.

Salina Coleman with her constant admirer, niece Kaliyah Coleman.

I can go on and on, but the fact is, despite what is unseen, God is in my life. "I may be living with Lupus but Lupus doesn't have me!" Lupus Awareness matters.

For more information, please visit www.lupus.org

Brooklyn Driver with a Genuine Heart

I've been disabled since 2006 and within those 17 years, I had to rely on different Ambulette Services to transport me to and from hospitals, clinics, rehabilitation facilities and adult day care centers.

The drivers I had were mostly Russian and/or Ukrainian. I also have had experiences riding with African, Haitian, Hispanic, West-Indian, and even an Asian driver.

It was not until I moved further into Bed-Stuy Brooklyn that I started to see more Afro-American drivers – drivers who are the same ethnicity as me!

Some drivers were not too friendly or courteous at all. Most failed to follow safety guidelines and state regulations. As an example, rogue drivers would speed up to beat the yellow light instead of slowing down. Others drove unsanitary vans, blasted music, or talked constantly on their cell phones while driving.

It was not until I took a specific Ambulette Service in late 2018, that I encountered the most pleasant, friendly, courteous, and most professional driver I had ever had! His name was Davis.

For the first time in years, I felt safe. Davis set the atmosphere for me. His van was very clean, and it smelled so good. He talked with much respect; he was very humble and quite funny. He made sure I was strapped in my chair securely. He always inquired about my comfort level and adjusted temperature levels to my liking.

What I loved most about Davis was the fact that he was not a speed demon! He drove carefully and that sat so well with me. My overall first ride with Davis at the wheel was very pleasant indeed! I decided, after that first experience, to have his company assigned as my permanent transportation service.

Days went to weeks; weeks went on to months and the months moved on to years.

During that time, I had a firsthand look at Davis in action and his interactions with other passengers. I observed how he treated them; asked how they were feeling; made sure they were strapped in, comfortably and securely; and always asked if they were okay. The bottom line: Davis cared for his passengers, especially his assigned dialysis patients.

That care could be seen in how he greeted them, took his time with them, and even went beyond the call of duty to lighten up their spirits if they were under the weather. I thought of him as the good Ambulette driver with a "Genuine Heart!" He did not regard his work as a heavy task or his passengers as a burden.

I found out that the best Ambulette drivers are underpaid and overworked! They squeeze in breaks just to eat, whenever they can. Davis even received back-to-back calls requesting pickups.

Sometimes, he dealt with hard-to-manage patients with bad attitudes. While he was driving, he often received calls from home health aides, medical assistants, and even some family members who wanted him to do things that were not in his job description. Nine times out of ten, Davis did his best to accommodate them. And he did that for me one late frigid evening.

I was the last drop-off at the end of what had probably been a long day for him. He often talked about his family, so I knew he was looking forward to getting home to share dinner with loved ones. His day usually began at 7:30 am, and sometimes he would work until 9:00 pm for the disabled, like me, and the elderly. Sometimes he missed personal time with his family before he got home.

Davis went beyond the call of duty, one evening, when I realized upon my arrival home, after a long ride, that I had left behind important documents that I needed for an appointment, the next morning.

Upon hearing of my dilemma, Davis's adrenaline kicked in. Ignoring my insistence that he should not worry, he said, "There's time. We're going back." The roundtrip ride from my residence to the site that was about to close, and my return home took at least an hour. But Davis was concerned that I would not be forced to cancel my next day's appointment at another site. We retrieved the medical documents, and he returned me safely to my home. For him, it was part of his job. But I knew it was not.

For me and countless others, Davis is Bedford-Stuyvesant's #1 ambulette driver, a caring, courteous, loving, hardworking individual in the community whose good deeds are not always acknowledged.

So, I am honored to recognize and show appreciation in this book for Davis, the Brooklyn Driver with a Genuine Heart of Gold. Thank you, Davis!

Salina Coleman

"GOD SAVED ME!"

Note to readers: I put my songs in poem form for my "Living with Lupus" testimonies in the hope that they minister to hearts and souls.

Listen very closely to this message just for you.

A message that is pure of heart, so precious and so true!

Back in the year 1996, something happened to me that I couldn't fix.

I was young at the time and incurred all the symptoms, but little did I know that I would be among its victims…

Going on with my life as if nothing was wrong, until I was diagnosed with LUPUS, so this is my song:

"GOD SAVED ME!"

LUPUS is a disease many people are not
    aware of!

You are frozen by fatigue; you start losing
    your hair.

A butterfly rash stains the bridge of your nose.

The fingertips turn yellowish and blue in
    the cold.

Joint pain starts in the morning, noon,
    and night.

Your eyes are sensitive to the sun and
    bright light.

Your body swells as big as can be!

I should know because it all has
    happened to me.

Found myself in SUNY Downstate Hospital
    in intensive care.

Being monitored closely and lost all my hair!

Tubes hanging from my body, I had to get
    a trach.

Could not walk, talk, or eat for six
    months straight.

I thought to myself, "Why me? This is
    not right.

"To be bedridden for months fighting for
    my life!

"I'm a good person. This is not fair!"

Yet, I kept the faith somehow,
    even though I was scared.

I see that God, in all his Glory, saved me...
    to tell the Story.

I want to thank my family, friends and all who
    prayed for me.

If it was not for God at the wheel, then
    "Where would I be?"

I give him all the PRAISE! He is real, you see.

He is saving my life.

He lives inside me.

My Rheumatologist

Twenty-six years ago, God sent an angel into my life.

Beautiful, soft-spoken, intelligent, caring, loving and hard-working, and a female doctor to boot.

Dr. Mona Pervil-Ulysses is my rheumatologist, and she is my friend!

In October 1996, I was receiving medical care at Interfaith Medical Center on Prospect Place in Brooklyn, New York and being treated for rheumatoid arthritis.

My condition had begun to worsen and all the treatments I was receiving at Interfaith were not working. I was in a critical state, on life support and headed to a fatal outcome. The hospital turned my charts over to its specialist in rheumatology: Dr. Pervil-Ulysses.

Despite my weakness, I was in awe of her when I saw her. Knowing I had a Black woman doctor put me at ease.

Little did I know at the time that she would turn out to be the earthly life support I needed, as well. She had just come into her rheumatology practice, and I was one of her very first Lupus patients. She quickly identified Lupus as my illness, an autoimmune disease that attacks the body's own immunity. This discovery immediately stopped the hospital from treating me for a condition I did not have.

Immediately, she knew exactly what tests and lab work needed to be done and what specialists I needed to see and what medications I needed to ingest.

I thank Him every day for placing Dr. Pervil-Ulysses in my life at the right time. She played a significant role in my health, and she has impacted my overall preventive care – and life – for more than a quarter century.

If it was not for her gifts and the Hands of God, I would not be alive today!

Dr. Mona Pervil-Ulysses (left) saw what no other physician detected. From the very first day we met in October of 1996 until this present time, I wouldn't trade her for anyone else. (Photo: Courtesy, S. Coleman)

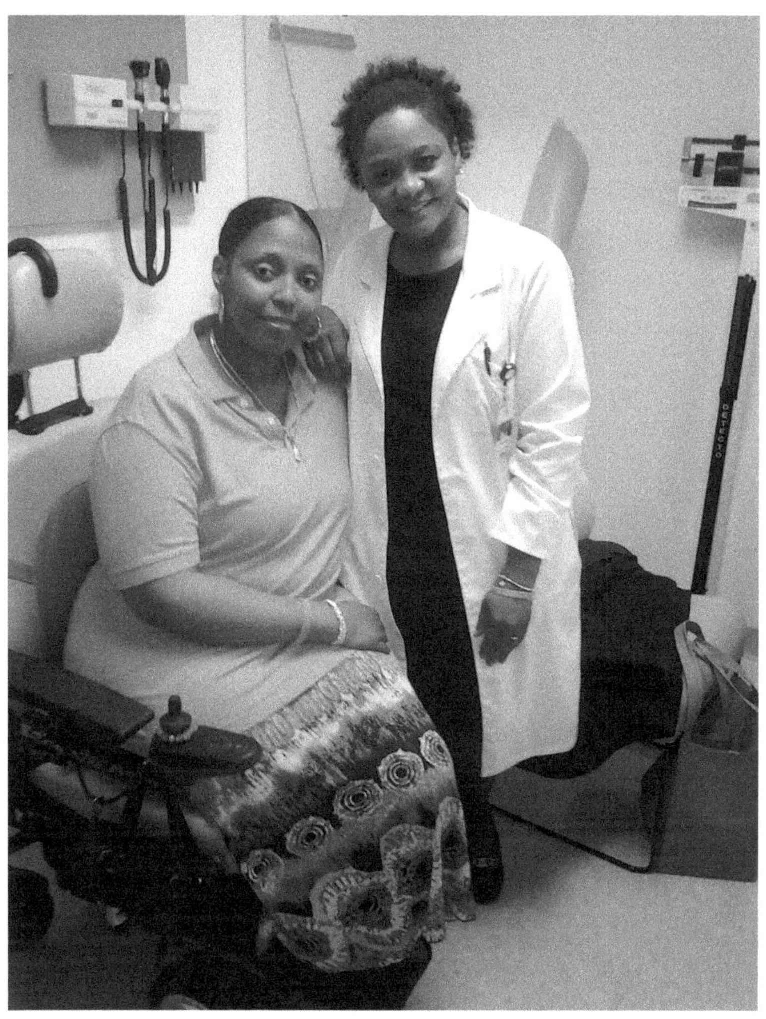

Dr. Mona Pervil-Ulysses (right) and Salina Coleman are friends for life through a bond sealed by faith and fueled by love and respect.
(Photo: Courtesy, S. Coleman)

CAROLE STEWART

Born August 1944 towards the end of World War II when bombs were bursting in air, Carole never made the connection until 9/11. "We sang The Star-Spangled Banner every day because we love our country, but the real meaning never came until the bombers were over our heads".

Fie Hankare

The Woman That I Am

My mom was a mom and home maker. Her day began with making breakfast, getting my dad off to work, and sending us out to school.

There were three of us: me, my sister, and my brother – the youngest, privileged and spoiled – we were charged to watch and take care of.

At some point, mom returned to work and my whole life changed. I, as a child, became a mom and teacher. I was responsible for making sure they completed their homework assignments, even when my siblings would lie and say, "We don't have any." *(I also was supposed to know when they were lying.)*

I was responsible for keeping the house clean; getting dinner started by the time mom came home; setting the table and making sure my siblings washed before dinner.

I always sent a thank you to Jesus when it was almost time for dad to arrive home.

My father was the gatekeeper, the peacemaker, and the head of the household. We all, including mom, listened when he spoke. His first words, coming through the door always were, "Is everyone okay?" In unison, we replied, "Yes, we are!"

Mom had us rehearse our reply to make sure it sounded believable. We were threatened, slapped, even beaten during rehearsal if our response didn't sound right. Her rationale? Dad worked hard and didn't deserve to come home to confusion and madness. So, we complied.

We learned to get through, and as we got older, we even learned to take care of each other.

Schools separated us. My siblings went to St. Emeric Catholic School, and I attended P.S. 34. Never knew why, but it always made me feel spited and the division between me and my siblings larger.

Soon after we all graduated, my dad became sick, and we used to sit and talk together. He asked me to take care of my mom, and make sure my baby sister finished college. I agreed. I did all he asked of me. Even married the man he chose for me. Regretfully.

Later, regaining my faith allowed me, a single mom, to appreciate and enjoy motherhood with my daughter and son. Then, my children gave me five beautiful grandchildren and a great grandchild to love and to cherish.

"Sorry for Your Loss"

I may never say those words because no matter how sincere you are: your sorry is just sorry.

Not because you don't feel or mean the words. They are inadequate, to say the least. You can only imagine what someone is feeling or going through. Even twins have different feelings for their parents. The only time I uttered those words, I ended up insulted and ashamed.

I was rendered a sermon, with choice words, about insensitivity and thoughtlessness for other people's feelings. I removed myself from the situation and never uttered those again.

I've since learned that no two hearts are alike, just as no two snowflakes or people are alike. God created each of us uniquely different and the same explicitly, and our beauty comes and shines from within our hearts. These are our emotions, and they create and cause all our emotions. These are the Beauties that attract us to each other or separate us from one another.

God created us all differently and the same: we all have hair, heads, necks, shoulders, chests, arms, hands, bellies, legs, feet, but none of us look the same. Factually, neither does anything that God spoke into existence or created. God is humorous, as well as very, very wise – to say the least.

COVID Within My Life

COVID separated my family members, physically. We couldn't visit each other for the first time since we were little, and it was the first time going through a hard time without my brother. He passed in September 2019 before COVID started. It made us rely on Duo, Zoom, group chat, and other social media.

It was my first Easter without a new Easter bonnet, a new pair of shoes, and a new dress. Vanity, it was truly all vanity. Around Resurrection Day 2020, the reality of thousands of people leaving the planet, suddenly all at once, settled in. Bodies in ice-trucks. Families and friends broken by the loss of loved ones, never having a chance to hold their hand or say goodbye. Everywhere was the same no matter what country you were in, the earth was full of dying people, of all ages everywhere. It was like a universal funeral, bowed heads, and sadness all over.

Then it was summer, but COVID still lingered. There were no cookouts, no concerts in the park, no traveling, no having friends over. We learned to truly trust God as there were no churches open. It's fall then winter and Christmas 2020. The younger members of the family set up zoom, at least we could see each other. East Coast, West Coast, and all in between. It was strange! Everyone was seated in front of laptops or cellphones, but the only aroma of food was what you cooked in your space.

There was none of the familiar aromas that come from holiday gatherings, especially cakes and pies. No gift-wrapping paper all over the floor, or the tables set up – one for adults, the other for the children and, of course, the children that reached the age to sit at the adult table. We just looked at each other, seeing the sadness but not talking about it.

Wow, we have come through another year. The schools re-opened. Vaccines have been found, but not everyone is trusting. The country is divided again. Hate has taken over again. No trust. No love. Not even between families.

We didn't do zoom this year, but we called each other, balancing out the time differences. Since Christmas, at least seven or more members of the family have encountered COVID, mild cases, but nonetheless, two children from different states brought it home from school, the others from work.

Thank God quarantine works, and no one had to be hospitalized. I find I pray more than ever before, as there is so much to pray about, including our World.

Thank God for Life!

TERRI MARDINA STROBERT

A writer at heart from the very start, Terri kept journals of her vacations and the interesting people she met starting out as a young lady from Brooklyn, New York.

Her biggest motivator was boredom so therefore, she stayed involved in activities of swimming, biking, dancing and researching all the while sharing her knowledge with others. Terri discovered she loved reading African American history and personal biographies. Her current passion is working in stained glass creating butterflies, sailboats, lamp shades and African statues. As a wife and mother, Terri loves entertaining and enjoying the company of family and friends.

Akoben

A Time for Change

A book report was due for my high school English class. It was my senior year and I was simply tired of the mundane tradition of choosing a book from the suggested reading list. I never finished reading a book and when I wrote my report, I bluffed my way through it. Sometimes I got caught, other times I didn't. The choices in reading materials were very limited and nothing interested me.

The country's current tumultuous crises resembles much of what was going on here more than 60 years ago. The Civil Rights Movement forced the nation to look at why Black Lives Matter then and now; there were demonstrations against racial inequities and protests to end The Vietnam War prevailed. Organizations like the Black Panther Party were poised to combat police brutality and push for healthier communities; visionary leaders like Malcolm X, then a spokesman for the Nation of Islam, advocated for Black empowerment. Turmoil and violence were all around us in the streets and in our communities.

Television, radio, and newspapers reported these stories daily. The difficulty was trying to make sense of it. We didn't quite understand what was going on and why. We were young and free-spirited with our lives ahead of us. The thought of being like our parents and taking on the burden and responsibilities of the world, wasn't what we teens looked forward to.

It all started to make sense when I entered Mrs. Horn's English class. As I approached her class for the first time, she stood outside of the classroom welcoming all the students. The way she looked seemed out of place as though she didn't belong there. She didn't wear makeup, dressed conservatively and lacked the frustrated, ruffled and rushed look. At first, I couldn't quite put my finger on it. Other students noticed it too, and then it hit me: she looked like a nun.

Yes! After eight years in a Catholic school, that was it. We found out that Mrs. Horn was a former nun and, boy oh boy, did the thoughts roam through our heads when the baby bump started showing. The jokes and giggles were going on secretly behind her back. Was Mr. Horn in fact "Father" Horn? When did he start tooting her horn? Did they get caught or just escaped in the middle of the night with a note left for Mother Superior? Had she broken her vows? Was it a mortal sin? Was she not a truly devout Catholic? I can just hear that famous phrase "May God Help You" when she told them she was leaving.

Mrs. Horn's real life story was better than any book I had read, and worthy of a report of some kind. I didn't know what to make of her until one day a couple of boys that sat up front of the class were involved in a serious conversation about a movie that they had seen. They were obviously influenced by it. So, when Mrs. Horn reminded us of the book report that was due, one of the boys asked her if he could write about this movie called "Easy Rider" about two "free wheeling hippies" on motorcycles from Southern California riding cross-country to the Mardi Gras in New Orleans. In the film, not only did these bikers use and sell drugs, they kept their stash safely hidden in their gas tanks. Throughout their treks through small southern towns, they encountered bigotry and hatred. They were jailed, chased by rednecks, shot and killed. "Easy Rider" was easy "coming-of-age" entertainment for some students, back then. So how could it not be the subject of a report?

The front section of the class began to share their opinions and were joined in by several other classmates who had seen the movie. Mrs. Horn was stunned and surprised. She was put on the spot and at a loss for words. She told the class that she and her husband would see the film and she would make a decision on the student's request.

With all the upheavals that Black Americans were going through, I could only imagine what went through the minds of my classmates – particularly those who saw parallels in the film between the treatment of the nonconforming white bikers and the racial attitudes and prejudices experienced by Black Americans had been subjected to and worse.

The following Monday, Mrs. Horn agreed to bend the rules, and she went a little further. Not only did she give a thumbs up to the student's request to write about "Easy Rider," she told the class that we could write about any movie or book that interested us.

So I decided to write about the movie titled "Anna Lucasta" starring Eartha Kitt in the title role and Sammy Davis, Jr. The story was about a preacher's daughter who wanted to become a professional singer. All she became was a nightclub singer in San Diego. Anna, played by Eartha Kitt, chose to live her own life and was disowned by her father and banned from the family. Her gigolo boyfriend, portrayed by Mr. Davis, only offered empty promises. But it was the loving care of her mother and sister who insisted that the father forgive her and allow Anna to come home.

Mrs. Horn gave my paper an A+, and, in reflecting back on those times and that experience it is the same grade I would give Mrs. Horn as a teacher. She was one of many unknown, outstanding education trailblazers.

The Woman In Me

In me, I am the thinker,
the dreamer and the writer.

I am the observer, the listener,
and the problem solver.

I am the seeker of knowledge,
the traveler ready to explore
exotic places.

I am a sponge who soaks it up
and rinses out the impurities
so, I can provide a sterile pathway
to possibilities.

I am the helping hand to all those
who share the quest for learning and
seeking knowledge to create a more
confident you.

I am the teacher, the parental guidance
to family and to the children of the future.

I am the accomplisher of love, happiness,
art, music and inspiration as I continue on
the pathway of my destiny enjoying the
journey of life.

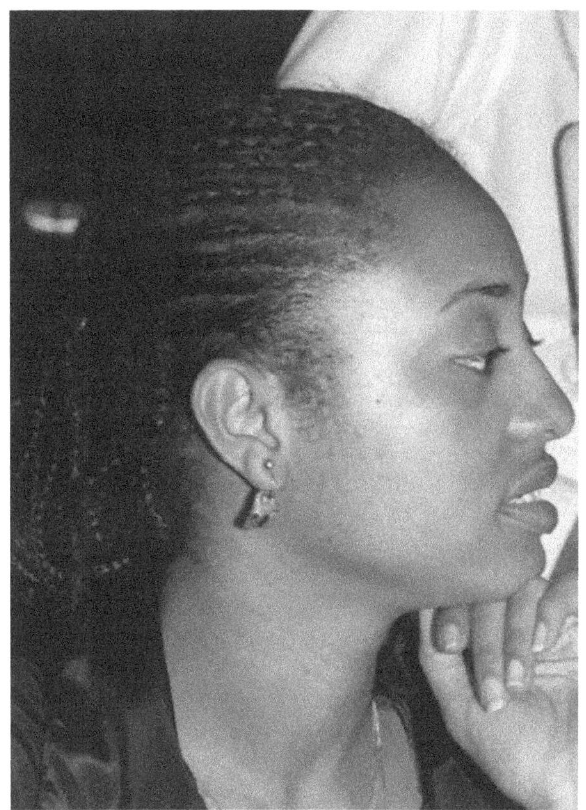

What a Great Surprise!

Tucked away in my memory bank, I was a child who never liked school but never had the heart to skip or play "hooky" as it was called back in the day. Those childhood feelings of not being seen or heard bothered me. Every time I tried to speak or tell a story, someone would interrupt me or simply change the subject. I didn't have a voice. No one cared about what I had to say. So, I decided I would learn to become like E.F. Hutton, the investor/stockbroker. When he spoke, everyone listened just like the commercial on television advertised. The United Negro College Fund advertised that "A mind is a terrible thing to waste" and my mother's words of wisdom were that "the only way to a better life is through an education". These past memories of advice turned into a reality.

In the spring of 2012, I picked up the after-school children from the neighboring public school. The kids had formed a two-line formation outside of the school and I had given permission to a few of them to buy icies from the street vendor selling nearby. Two brothers waiting in line, Kamal and Kevin began calling out to a boy walking towards the school. "Yo ... Raheem" Kamal called out. "Raheem" Kevin, his younger brother, shouted out. "What's up?" they asked, greeting each other smiling and exchanging the clench fist pound to pound handshake.

After the icies were bought, we proceeded to walk the one block to the church where the program was held. Raheem changed his mind from entering the school and began walking and talking with the brothers who had shown so much admiration for him. "He's my cousin," Kamala said, smiling as we walked on. "Cousin?" Makaela asked with a questioning look on her face. Then someone shouted out "they're not cousins, they're friends". Kamala started laughing knowing he got caught telling a story.

Suddenly, Makaela quietly called me over and whispered "Ms. Marshall, see that boy, he never comes to school." I glanced over to take a look at him and realized that I had seen him before and her comment about him sounded familiar. "You told me this before, Makaela," I answered. I said nothing more about the eleven- or twelve-year-old boy still walking along with his friends as we headed towards the church.

He was probably in the fourth or fifth grade and I couldn't help thinking why did she keep telling me this. She didn't know there was nothing I could say or do. I didn't know him and he wasn't in the program. As a rule, teachers and childcare providers are careful about prying into the privacy of children. The law mandated that you report any suspicious negligence to the proper authority.

Before I could think another thought about the matter, Makaela's voice drowned out everyone's when she asked out loud "Raheem! why don't you come to school?"

The look of surprise fell across his face as his eyes stretched wide showing that he was caught off guard as did everyone else. All eyes turned to look at him. Silence fell momentarily and not a sound could be heard as we waited anxiously for his answer. "I hate school" he said angrily! "The teachers get on my damn nerves!" She paused and then said, "So what do you do all day?"

Raheem had everyone's attention. His body movement suggested that he was trying to relax a little as he spoke about the television shows on Cartoon Network and Nickelodeon including the video games he played. He started naming some of his favorite games such as Super Smash Brother, which got him a loud cheer from the kids, Batman Ankham City and the NBA 2K13 basketball video game. David yelled out "Oh snap! I got that game too."

Wait...a minute, I thought to myself, observing that all the kids had become mesmerized with smiles on their faces that grew bigger and bigger. This was my cue to get involved. "Young man" I said, "you think you're having a good time but you're hurting yourself." I spoke to him about getting older, being left behind while friends and everyone else would have moved on with their life. I mentioned his ability to find a job instead of standing on some street corner all day long. I ended with "do your parents know what you're doing?" He ignored me and kept on talking about the games and television shows. I interrupted him once again, repeating what I said adding this "you will be in the same grade as a grown man".

Suddenly, Kevin, the youngest of the two brothers told a joke, "Yeah, Ms. Marshall, twenty-two and still in the second grade". Everyone started laughing. I was stunned. Amazed by what I just heard. On Raheem's face came the second look of surprise. His eyes stretched wide and I could see that he got the message with a little help from his friend as he slipped away from us and went into the park.

I was rather proud of eight year old Kevin. His words of wisdom came out of the mouth of a babe. I didn't realize how inquisitive and observant Makaela was with so much boldness and courage to spark a conversation between Raheem and herself. Kevin, indeed, tied it all together with his powerful statement.

My thoughts remained on Raheem for a few days as I looked for him in passing when I picked up the kids from school. Finally, I saw him. This time it was in reverse. Raheem was leaving school, walking and talking with a friend carrying his book bag on his back.

I felt proud of him that he made his own decision, possibly prompted by an adult, to go back to school.

Makaela became the voice of E.F. Hutton that sparked an interest in Raheem. We all listened to her loud and clear, and Kevin provided a reality whereas a mind that was about to be lost was saved. I believe Raheem will always have this experience to tuck away in his own memory bank.

Terri Mardina Strobert

DEBRA A. JOHNSON

Manhattan-born Debra A. Johnson is a community advocate and expert in the development of positive life-enhancement strategies and tactics for individuals, groups, and communities – from Central Brooklyn to Ghana, where she currently lives.

A recipient of a Dual Masters in Human Development and Social Change, Ms. Johnson has realized two main life goals, among her many other achievements: the childhood dream of living on the Mother Continent and the establishment of a major positive initiative that is a catalyst for global change: Support Motivate Invest Love Educate (SMILE).

Ms. Johnson's initiative is anchored in the concept of sharing. She believes we all were born with unique gifts to share for the purpose of building our individual selves, our communities, and our global cultures.

"The process starts with asking yourself, 'What do you love doing so much that you would do it without compensation?' She believes that it is never too late to learn how to share your gift. SMILE is designed to help."

Gye Nyame

Dream Delayed: America to Africa

My mother, Mazarina David Johnson, told me in 2021 with tears in her eyes: "Debbie, I am so glad I lived to see you fulfill your dream of living in Africa. You have been talking about Africa since you were 15 years old."

I was clear at a very early age that I was an African born in 1953 in America.

In 2018, at age 65, I was blessed to travel to my homeland Ghana, West Africa in the Volta Region. Deep in my soul, I felt it was a calling. I never really felt comfortable in America.

The journey turned out to be a rebirth for me and a more meaningful connection to my roots.

Born on sharecropper's land in Wagram, North Carolina in 1933, mom was the 19th born of 20 (documented births). Her brother was born four years later (only 12 siblings survived to adulthood). In 1940 when her father died, since there was no male child old enough to work the crops, they had to leave the land. My grandmother was now a single parent at age 50.

With six of her younger children in tow, my grandmother moved from Wagram, North Carolina, to Manhattan, New York to live with one of my mother's older sisters. In addition to the children, my grandmother brought a taste of the deep south (our Africa roots) to the city.

Growing up, I was torn between two continents – Africa and North America. At the time, I did not know which part of Africa's

54 countries I was from; I only knew "The Motherland" was where I belonged.

My parents married in 1952 in "The City." A year later, I made my grand entrance into the world – the only one of their brood born in New York. In 1955, we moved to Cleveland, Ohio where the rest of my siblings were born.

Life circumstances delayed me from fulfilling my dream, yet I never gave up. While in Cleveland, I remember as a young child when I was about age 9, I told my mother: *"I think I am adopted because I do not feel right."* She was hurt yet she assured me I was not adopted. My parents separateed when I was 10 making my mother a single parent at age 29. Now two generations!

As the oldest of five, I became the sibling co-parent of my three brothers and my sister. I was angry most of the time because of the responsibility. I survived by keeping busy.

To fill the void and release the anger, I escaped through my made-up plays, track, roller skating, swimming, and other activities. Reading books took me to places I had never been. Sometimes, I would run to my bedroom closet where darkness pacified and caressed me, and mentally transported me away from everyone and everything; it felt surreal, like I was floating in space.

I loved going to movies and would imagine myself as one of the characters. Rainy days were and still are soothing, my heaven on Earth. I played in the warm rain; it was so refreshing and freeing. The theater and playing school were also escape outlets. The world was my stage!

I attended Jane Addams, an all-girls vocational high school in Cleveland, Ohio. I became a pretty good seamstress. At age 14, while still in school, I was still caring for my younger brothers and sister, still getting in trouble for their wrong doings and mine. It was overwhelming. I could not breathe. I felt the only road to happiness was to run as fast as I could to Milwaukee, Wisconsin (1971) to live with my father, who I had not lived with in over 10 years. It was the path to freedom. Or so I thought.

I enrolled in a Drama Class at the University of Wisconsin (UWM) Extension Theater Company. I quit the theater when I was called to work for The Telephone Company (unaware that I could do both). My first child was born in 1973 with the hopes the baby's arrival would fill the void I felt inside. A year later, I transferred to California with my job at the telephone company to follow the father of my child in his search for his dad. Dreams deferred again!

I was involved in a serious near fatal car accident as a pedestrian in October 1975; it almost ended my dreams.

In May 1978, I married the father of our five-year-old daughter who was our flower girl. We bought our first home in December of that year. I was 25 and the only one holding down a job.

Three years later and six months pregnant, in September 1981, my husband and I opened, financed, and operated a combo Beauty Supply store and Beauty Salon. Four months later in December, we were juggling marriage, a home, a child, a business and giving birth to our second daughter. Dreams deferred again.

It was a blessing when my mother moved in with us and helped with the Beauty Supply/Salon and the children, since I was working a full-time job as the main financial provider. The yearning for something more persisted. I recalled a line from a sermon I had heard: *"A bell is not a bell until you ring it, and love is not love until you give it."* That hit home!

When I was using my talents and having children, *I felt at the time it was love* and a life saver while yet still feeling trapped, never really feeling free, never feeling "at home". I got involved with my children's schools and became very active in the community. Then, I had an epiphany thinking having another child was the key. We had our son in 1984.

By 1987, my husband left, and I became a single parent (now three generations). I started traveling within the United States: taking cruises, going to Hawaii, Disney World, Nevada, Mexico and more. I was like a nomadic herdswoman: wandering, wandering,

wandering. I made bad choices, in search of better – in search of me.

After working hard for over 34 years, raising a family, owning a home, and starting a business, I wanted to be free and continue to travel. I truly believed the more I learned and traveled, the more choices and freedom I would have, all the while gaining wisdom. I felt that after taking care of everyone else, it was time to Do Me, Love Me!

I earned my dual master's in human development/social change from Pacific Oaks College, CA in 2012, at 59 years old. The course was titled *The Game Has Changed: Teaching and Learning with The First Digital Generation.*

Then, two years later, I was working toward my PsyD/MFT at the college when I had kidney surgery. I took a leave of absence from school, and never returned.

I continued my work in the community and schools with SMILE, but I was still yearning, still searching. After all my children left home, I was finally free to do me.

In 2016, I decided to do my family research through Ancestry.com – first on my mother Mazarina (David) Johnson and, a year later, on myself. The results were similar. Our connection was 80% African, with the concentration in Ghana and Cameroon, and 14% Irish.

For me, those findings shed light on the answer to my lifelong question of "Why I felt out of place in America."

Debra A. Johnson

America to Africa

In May 2018, with a backpack and a prayer, I took a leap of faith and travelled to Ghana (Home!), landing in the West African nation's Ho Municipal District in the Volta Region.

My son introduced me via Internet to a person he met while on a mission in Ghana in 2011 (seven years earlier). His Ghanaian contact walked me through the process online and over the phone regarding Visas, yellow fever shot, malaria pills, sponsor letters and other useful knowledge. The gentleman also told me: "Don't just pass through Ghana allow Ghana to pass through you." I took that to heart.

After taking care of my affairs in the states, I arrived in Accra, the capital of Ghana on May 1, 2018 then made the ardurous 4½ hour drive to the Vola Region, Ho where I stayed with a family of seven, that I now call my "Angel Family". As soon as I hit the soil, I knew I was home.

I stayed with them for 30 days and slept on a foam mat on the floor, with no hot running water and one bathroom. Because of their genuine outpouring of love, these accommodations felt like a five-star hotel. I was in tears. The family was so kind and as an Elder I was treated like a Queen. They did not allow me to do anything. They washed my clothes by hand, cleaned my room, shopped and cooked for me. They did it all with an abundance of love.

What really struck me was seeing my people everywhere: on the billboards, television, owning their own businesses and homes. I was impressed that even the currency Cedis (GHS) had our faces on it. The food was amazing from the peas and rice, okra stew, light soup, banku, Tilapia, red mangos, papaya, avocado, white yams, bananas, plantain, and my first coconut water straight from the tree. Market Day every four days, it was the hightlight of MY week experiencing the blended cultures, languages, food artistry, dress, beauty and more. This facinated ME. I found myself immersed in the culture, different languages, and the sheer beauty of it all. Sometimes I would just observe, No Shopping Necessary.

I believe it is more important to first absorb the culture and learn about the currency, the rest comes easier. I went to Ghana to retire not as a tourist. I spoke to hundreds of students from kindergarten to high school, in the Volta Region where they speak Ewe and British English.

In the area where I stayed, most of the farming families' children who attended public school from KG-1 & KG-2 through 4th grade were encouraged to attend school for the free hot meals. For some that meal was the only one of the day.

I chose to learn the language and culture from the KG-1 and KG-2. I was inspired by the children's thirst for their education despite their learning environment: some classes had no walls; students carried their desks and benches to class; chalkboards and rocks – not technology – were used to learn their lessons, there was no running water and students had to bring their own lunch bowls, spoons, and water cups.

There was no inside plumbing – they had to use outhouses; yes, outhouses. I did not like the Corporal Punishment canes which were used to punish the children and were sold in the school supply stores and at the Market.

In the public schools, both girls and boys wore uniforms and I was told they kept their heads shaved for health reasons.

In Ghana, you are considered an Elder at age 60. I truly admired the respect most Ghanaians have for their Elders and the village/community concept.

In Volta Region, Senior Convalescent (nursing) homes do not exist; the families and/or the village take care of the Elders.

Do not get me wrong, there are pros and cons in Ghana; but, for me, the pros outweigh the cons. There are 16 regions in Ghana, about 40 languages and more than 100 dialects. Most students are bilingual with British English being the universal language. Some of the natives know four languages Ewe, English, French, and Twi.

I love Ghana. I have been traveling back and forth to the West African nation since 2018. Now, I want to leave a legacy. I want to travel, document, and share the SMILE 'til the day I die.

This Dream Delayed was worth it. I am home.

HOME

I am 'Home.'

I cannot describe the feeling of Joy in
    my bones.

I feel the Joy and the Pain

Tears for my Ancestors who were slain.

We were not animals nor born "Slaves."

Some were Kings, Queens, Teachers, Doctors,
    Mothers, Fathers, Lawyers...and more,

Stripped and locked down in chains.

Torn from families and much more,

to this day it is a pain we bear.

"We" were/are NOT IMMIGRANTS.

I am an African Queen; you can see my inner
    calling has set me Free.

From 1619, snatched from Ghana in chains,
    I was treated less than human with Royalty
    in my veins.

I am proud to be home and to feel so free.

Living in a hut in Africa is better than a
    mansion...in America,

To me.

It is home.

I am free.

DARCELLA JONES

A native New Yorker, Ms. Jones, a fine artist, has resided in Brooklyn all her life. As a retired senior, she is exploring, "with passion," her life-long interest in the fine arts and arts & crafts. Examples of her drawings and paintings are displayed throughout this book, which reflects her interpretations of the writing work of her Tompkins Park sister-scribes. As a self-described writing novice, Ms. Jones, a natural storyteller, has shared that writing is the one art form she never thought she could attempt. She hails the workshop for giving her the opportunity to "incorporate true-life personal stories into fictional stories," an art she says that despite its demands, she "enjoys very much." Ms. Jones also recently resurrected her interest, since childhood, in sewing, knitting, crocheting and other varieties of crafts. She loves travelling in the U.S. and abroad, and, at home, in Brooklyn, she likes to line-dance and still roller skates.

My Sisters

It's going to be a bright sunny day. Warmer than usual for this time of the year, so the weatherman said. My younger sister, Ellen, was so excited this morning about starting college. She wanted to go away to school but we just could not afford it. Pa passed away but left us enough money to keep us going for a while. We were still waiting for the insurance policy to kick in. My sister Betty was still in mourning. For several months, she had been laying on the couch, watching TV all day in her pajamas, eating up everything in the house. I have not said anything to her yet.

Betty was always my father's favorite. Whenever Betty did something dumb, Pa would laugh and say, "She just trying to find herself." Ellen and I would look at each other and just roll our eyes. I'm the oldest and with Pa gone I know I must take charge. Ellen, the baby of the family, was no problem. She will do whatever I say. But that Betty is another story!

Ma died several years ago. She had breast cancer, that was in remission. Then it spread into her lungs. She never complained. She would always talk to me and show me how to run the house. She told me, "Sam you're a big girl now even though you're only 14 years old". When I was at home, I stayed by Ma's side. I did everything she did. She even taught me how to budget the money for the house and go to the bank. After a while, Pa started giving me his pay at the end of the week. I would make out the checks to pay the bills. When I finished, I showed Ma and she would sign the checks. Ma would say "Sam you're doing just fine. You can run this house by yourself." I was so proud of myself.

I began to boss my sisters around. Betty was two years younger than me, but she would never listen. I would get so mad at her. I called out to ma, "Betty won't listened to me". Ma told Betty, "You have to listen to your older sister. Betty would just stick her tongue out at me and keep on going. Ma told me, "Be patient she'll come around".

After Ma died several years ago, Pa didn't seem to care about anything. Not even us. After the funeral, Aunt Frieda stayed with us for a while. She would say, "It's going to be alright girls". Pa just had to find a way to get over his hurt. I felt lost without Ma around. I knew she wanted me to be the woman of the house now.

Aunt Frieda was Pa's oldest sister and the one that was always around. She lived down the road with her husband Jesse and their four children. Although Pa had four sisters and three brothers, Aunt Frieda was my favorite. Pa had to leave early every morning for work. He would wake me up before he left. It was my job now to wake my sisters up in the morning and make sure they were dressed for school. When they came downstairs, I made sure breakfast was on the table: a box of cereal and cold milk. We all had cereal of our choice. I gave each one their lunch money before we were off to school.

When we came home from school, we knew that Aunt Frieda had been there. She straightened up the house and left dinner on the stove. She always left a note with instructions; for example, "Get the dirty clothes together so I can wash them tomorrow." We would change from our school clothes to our play clothes and settle down to do our homework. When Pa came home from work, we would quiet down. We set the table for dinner and waited for Pa to eat. We could not eat until Pa blessed the food. At the table we would talk about our day and sometimes argue with each other. Things seemed different now, there were times that Pa seemed far away in thought. When dinner was over, we all chipped in to wash and put away the dishes. Soon after, Pa would tell us it was bedtime. I would make sure my sisters washed up and were ready for bed. Pa would check in on us. He made sure we said our prayers together, just like Ma did. He tucked us in and gave us a good night kiss before turning out the lights.

One day, Betty refused to do what I asked. We got into a big argument. Betty yelled, "You're not Ma". I said, "I know, but Ma left me in charge". When I went to bed, I cried all night. It finally hit me that Ma was gone forever. Pa too was finish with his hurt and he started taking care of us. I helped and he still let me handle the money as always.

After a year or so, Pa started dating. On the weekends, he would polish his shoes, take out a clean white shirt from the Chinese laundry, put on his good suit, splash on some Old Spice, and put us to bed before going out. Aunt Frieda would babysit. I would try to stay awake until he came home. When he came in, I would crack the bedroom door open and listen to him and Aunt Frieda talking. She would ask him if he had a good time. He said yes and talk about this lady. I believe they knew each other for a long time. Her name was Sarah. When they finished talking, I'd tip toe back to bed. Pa looked in on us and I pretended to be asleep.

It was several months before Pa introduced Sarah to us. I didn't tell my sisters that I knew about her. She was pretty alright, but she only had one arm. The first thing we asked her was what happen to your arm. She said, she lost it in a bad car accident. We could not understand why Pa would go out with a one arm woman. Over time Ellen grew to really like her. But Betty and I were not having it. This was the first time both of us could agree on something. We called her Miss Thing. A couple of times Pa pulled us to the side and said, "be nice to Sarah". We said OK. But Betty and I did everything we could to make sure she didn't come back.

Aunt Frieda sat us down one day and tried to explain how it was with a man and woman. She said our father needed someone. I didn't understand at the time because he had us. I told her that

Ma made me the lady of the house and I wasn't going to have someone else stepping in. Aunt Freida raised her voice and said, "Samantha, that's not nice, you're just a kid". When Aunt Frieda was mad at me, she called me Samantha just like Ma did. Pa and Sarah dated for a couple of years. I think Pa had an argument with her one day about us and we never saw her again. Years later after Pa died, I had regrets that we did not let him find true happiness again. I kept this to myself.

Betty finally got up off the couch this morning and cleaned herself up without me saying a word. She came into the room just to talk. She told me how she felt. She was afraid and sad that our parents were gone. I told her I felt the same way. She thanked me for taking over after our parents had died. She said, she didn't know what she would have done without me. Right then, we embraced each other and cried together. Ellen came in the room with her bubbly self; asking, "Hey...what's going on?" She saw us hugging and joined in.

For the first time we said how much we loved each other. From that day on we became very close. Sisters protecting each other. I remember my Ma saying, "Just be patient. She'll come around."

Grandma

Grandma Sage loved to sit in her rocking chair, next to the fireplace, holding her Bible. She had been blind for most of her adult life. But she could feel things that most of us cannot see. The radio was always turned on to a religious station.

She lived in a small one-story wood frame house with a tin roof and a porch. The house only had two bedrooms, even though her parents had twelve children. Grandma said she grew up in this house. The house that her father built.

Down the road is the Middlebrook Plantation. Her father was a slave on that plantation. He raised and groomed horses for Master John Middlebrook. Grandma said her father was Master John's son. Although Master John never admitted it, he gave her father five acres of land after the Civil War ended. Her Pa was free, but he still worked for Master John because he was the best horse groomer in South Carolina.

As a child, Grandma picked cotton at Middlebrook to help her family. She said it was hard work especially in the hot sun. If you did not pluck the round, fluffy bolls of cotton from its rough casing just right, your fingers could be cut or pierced. This work prevented her from going to school. She did not learn how to read nor write until she was an adult.

Christ Church Parish is the small black community that we live in. Most of the people that lived here are related and/or good friends. Their parents or great-grandparents were also slaves for Master John. After the Civil War, they did not venture out very far from the plantation. Since each had a different talent, they used their unique gifts to build a community: houses, a church, a community center and a school. The general store they built was run by a white family and it still is.

Everyone called grandma, Mama Sage. Someone was always stopping by the house. They brought food or took her to church on Sundays which she tried never to miss. She has been attending New

Hope Baptist Church since she was a child. She sang in the choir and didn't need a hymn book. She knew almost every song and many times they let her sing solo. On special occasions, she let me sing with her. If she was unable to go to church, the preacher would stop by with a couple of members to see how she was feeling. Before they left, they would begin to pray. The house would be filled with the sounds of singing, praying, and talking in tongues for hours.

If she had to go somewhere during the week, she would get dressed, put on her favorite hat, grab her black pocketbook, and stand by the side of the road. Someone always would stop, pick her up and take her wherever she had to go. She never went far. She repeated this method to get back home.

My mama was her only child, and I am her only grandchild. We visited grandma at least twice a week. When I came into the house, she would say, "Child is that you, Emoni?" I would reply, "Yea, Granny". Then she would say, "Come over here, baby. Let me take a good long look at you." She would take both of her hands and feel every inch of my face. Especially my eyes, nose and around my lips. Then she would put her hands on my shoulders giving me a big, long hug and a squeeze. She would say, "Girl, you're getting so big!" and we would both laugh. I asked her, one day, "Why do you feel my face every time I come?" She laughed and said, "Baby, I don't want to forget what you look like."

When we were alone, Grandma would ask me what's the matter, or why was I so happy. Like a fortune teller, she could sense something was going on with me. I would tell grandma everything. It was our little secret. She would give me advice that always helped me out. Then she would have me read something from the Bible. She knew exactly what book, chapter, and verse in the bible she wanted me to read. She would tell me to remember that bible verse. It will help you out of your problems and then thank God for his help. Then she would rock back and forth in her chair singing: "Have a little talk with Jesus. Tell him all about your troubles."

Grandma told me she was a well-known Jazz and Blues singer back in the day. She sang in many cities and towns, like New York and Chicago and juke joints in the south. She loved to sing and always sang to me. One of the songs she loved to sing was "St. Louis Blues." She told me I was too young to understand it. I knew every word and I would join in with her when she sang that song. She said, I was a good singer.

At home, I would walk around the house singing, "St. Louis woman with her diamond rings." Ma would stop me. She said the song was too grown for me to sing. I always responded, "But Grandma taught it to me." She always answered, "I know." Grandma had taught her that Bessie Smith song when she was younger, too. When Ma was not around, I sang it as loud as I could as I switched around the house. It made me feel good.

Grandma told me when she was around 30 years old, she got sick. It took several weeks before the doctor could come see her. The midwife did all she could to keep her alive. No one knew what was wrong with her. A year later she lost her sight, but she never let that keep her down. "Life is too short," she said.

After finishing high school, I went to a local college. When I graduated, Grandma insisted that I move away. She said, "See the world! This town is too small and it's not for you." Ma didn't want me to go. But I listened to Grandma and eventually moved to New York which I loved. It was just how Grandma described it, "Exciting."

So, now, I am following in Grandma's footsteps. I got a job singing in night clubs. I came home two or three times a year. I wrote often. I knew Ma would read my letters to her. Even though Grandma was blind, she was wise and could see so much.

Grandma died at the age of 98. I missed her touching my face and our long secret talks. I still love to sing that old blues song. I sing it every time I think of her. Mama said that song reminded Grandma of a love that she lost. I guess that's why I love it, too.

SELMA JACKSON

Fulfilling a childhood dream, Selma Jackson, quit her job as a banker to pursue a promise to herself to own a business after age 40! The result: 4W Circle of Art & Enterprise, Inc., came forth, and served the community for 17 years. In retirement, Ms. Jackson authored two children's books (her first, "GRANNY'S HELPER", was winner of Young Readers Award in Harlem Book Fair), is an advocate for Brooklyn seniors and church volunteer. She is in her 8th year as the creative writing facilitator of the Tompkins Park Senior Center Advisory Council and was elected President of the Age Friendly Central Brooklyn, Inc. Board of Directors in June 2020. Ms. Jackson says her family and friends sustain her. She treasures her son, three grandchildren and great-grandson.

Adinkrahene

Shoe Sisters

It was not easy having big feet. I had the unfortunate or maybe fortunate fate of inheriting my father's.

Growing up, my shoe size matched my age until I reached 12.

At age 10, I remember my fifth grade was getting ready to study Argentina. My teacher, Ms. Pierce, described Argentina "as the land of the big feet," and everyone in the class turned around and looked at me. I wanted to crawl into a hole or at least disappear from my desk.

At the beginning of the sixth grade, my family moved, but since it was my final year at P.S. 63, my parents let me graduate with my classmates and friends who I had known since first grade.

Not only was I going to attend a new school the following year, but my parents had decided that even though they were not able to buy a house in the North Bronx, they would still send me to a school in that neighborhood. It was then called voluntary bussing. The school was so far away that I took a 30-minute train ride each way. My first day of school at the new junior high school changed my life forever.

I was shy, self-conscious, and very apprehensive about being picked on because of my big feet. I entered my new classroom and sat in the last seat of the first row. I was able to observe all of the students who entered the room, and I looked at the feet of each girl. Suddenly, I smiled. One of the girls entered the room with a pair of shoes that I knew were purchased at the shoe store I went to (the choice of shoe stores was limited back in the 1950's). I knew because I had tried on a pair there and didn't get them because they looked like boats on my feet!!

The first chance I got, I introduced myself to Judith and asked her if she got her shoes from Tall Gals. She answered yes. Elated, I shared with her that I shopped there as well. That night, we told our mothers that we had found someone else in class who had big feet! Judith told her mom that my feet were bigger than hers and I told my mom that Judith shopped at "our" shoe store.

By the end of the week, we had found two other girls in the class that had big feet. Our protective circle included Sheila, Pamela, Judith and me or 10, 11, 11½ and 12! To belong to our group, you had to wear a size 10 or larger. By having our group no one picked on us about our feet. We were inseparable throughout junior high school.

We could not wear the Fred Braun or Clark shoes, but we were included in the social mix.

In the ninth grade, Sheila moved to White Plains, NY and her parents did the same thing as mine had done. Sheila commuted daily for her last year, and we all graduated together.

By high school, Pamela separated from the group, but Judith and I remained close. After school we would go to the Evander Sweet Shop almost every day. We called one another at home often and our parents eventually became friends. Judith stayed over at my house, and I stayed at her home. We were like sisters.

Since we shopped at the same shoe store we began shopping together. Judith's foot is narrow so we rarely wore the same style, but we would make suggestions to one another on which shoe to buy. That proved to be very important later in life. We graduated from high school together and remained friends. We were inseparable.

During our second year in college, Judith got married and, because her husband was in the military, moved from The Bronx to Omaha, NE. Unfortunately, there were no large-size shoe stores within driving distance of the state. So, for the four years she was in Omaha, I would meet her mom at Tall Gals in Manhattan, and we would go shoe shopping for Judith and me. I tried on the styles that she liked, and her mom would decide if they would work for Judith. I also weighed in on the selection since I knew what my friend liked as well. Judith's next move was Detroit and while she was finding her way around the motor city identifying shoe stores, her mom and I continued to shoe shop for her in New York.

Judith still lives in Detroit and, of course, our favorite experience is shoe shopping wherever we may be! But now we get to experience it with a new generation, as footage continues to grow in our families.

Judith has two daughters. One wears size 10 shoes and has done so since age 10. As an understanding "Auntie", I consoled her on what she believed was a downside of having big feet. I let her know the upside of her inheritance: they were the catalysts for her mom and I becoming good friends and going the distance in our lives.

I was blessed with a boy. I say blessed with a boy because it doesn't become difficult to find shoes for boys until after their feet reach size 15. As an adult, he currently wears a 14.

Now, Judith and I are both grandmothers and, so far, it seems she may not have a foot problem with her grandchildren. My first grandchild is Emani and her feet appear to be growing like mine did. When she was 10, she wore size 10 shoes. At first, she appeared uncomfortable with her feet almost as if she wanted to disappear. I saw the self-consciousness and when I visited, I took her shoe shopping and shared that I had the same "big" challenge growing up.

Her sister, Jourdan, who is two years younger, also has large feet; they both are now wearing size 12. Since they are military kids and have moved often, being able to talk about all the nuances accorded feet and shoe sizes with trusted family members is a big help. Emani and Jourdan are supporting each other in this shoe experience. Their brother wears size 14 shoes and is still growing at 17.

So, this story is, no pun intended, expanding. There may be an addendum. Meanwhile, the footnote is: Judith and I have been close friends for 60 years and we enjoy telling people it all happened over shoes.

My Sister Jean

My sister Jean was my Shero. We were 9 years apart but she was my go-to person despite our age differences.

My first remembrance was preschool. My cousin who lived with us was speaking to her sister and asked her to go get a box of M-o-d-e-s-s. I go running to Jean and asked, "What's m-o-d-e-s-s?" Jean, surprised. responds with a question: "Where did you hear that?" I said, "Evelyn was speaking to Barbara." Jean told me what it was and showed one to me. Just as fast as I found out I promptly forgot about it!

We lived on Boston Road and my school, family and friends were across the street. It was a wide street and I had not yet learned to cross. Whenever I needed to get to the other side, Jean would cross me. I would wait for the signal hand motion and run to where she was. One such time changed our lives: June 28, 1951. I had finished school and was waiting for Jean to give the signal. I saw her hands waving, I run and I am hit by a car. I am frightened and get up and am nearly hit by a second car. An ambulance comes to get me. By God's Grace, I had minor injuries and was released the next day. Children had been killed crossing Boston Road! Once I was well enough to go out again the first thing Jean taught me was how to cross a street!

Our apartment is on the front of our building and Mom sees all of this from the window. She's expecting a baby and she's rushed to the hospital because she starts to have pain and it's a month early.

My dad comes home from work, rushes to the hospital to see me in the children's ward and my mother in the maternity ward! My baby sister, Beverly, was born that day!

Despite our age difference all of my friends had to meet my sister. It was as if I was her daughter and she gave approval of my friends through middle school, high school and college!

So, you can imagine when I am 27 years old and Jean stops speaking to me, I am devastated!! I call her several times only for her to hang up and finally not to answer at all!!

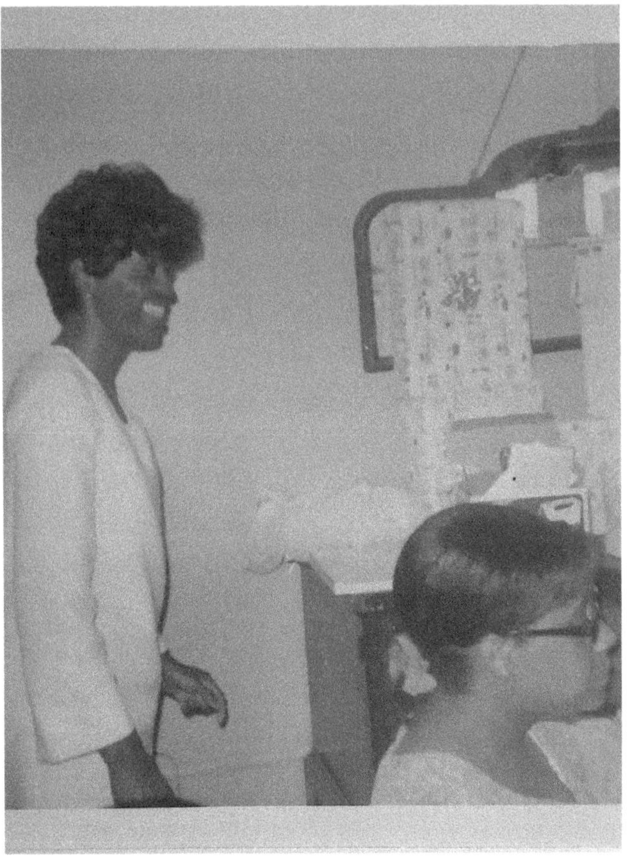

Our parents had separated. As painful as it was, I felt we needed to be supportive of their decision. Of the five of us, I was the only one who felt that way. Two supported my mom and two supported my dad. I was the middle child of five girls and I was in the middle on this.

Four of us were married at the time, my baby sister was in college. There was no reasoning with anyone. My sibling relationships changed forever that year!

Three years later, my dad dies of diabetic complications! Six months after my dad's death, Jean and her four children are murdered in Teaneck, NJ! I go for therapy and struggle with the question: would my sister still be alive if we had continued to talk?

In 1991, sixteen years after the death of my father, sister, two nieces and two nephews, I open a business in Fort Greene, Brooklyn with three friends. That business lasts for 17 years. My mother died three months after closing the business. I start therapy again and the therapist suggests I write a letter to my sister.

In writing the letter I discovered that one of the reasons for starting the business was to create a safe environment for minority businesses – sparing them the need to borrow money from loan sharks. My sister's husband had gotten his financing for their home and his business that way and wasn't able to make his payments.

Although it was difficult to relive that experience of great loss, I was overwhelmed with joy that brought me to tears with an enlightening revelation: through 17 years of business ownership, I had actually paid tribute to my sister, Jean.

My Hands

I've always been conscious of my hands as I write, as I carry things, and as I cook. They're always there to help me.

I'm often queried about whether I play the piano. I attempted to learn once at 39 and again at 59. I think I'll try again. Start, then stop; start, then stop. And then start again. Oops–I don't have a nine in my age this time. Hope that might make the difference!

I am thankful for my hands to help me create desserts for family and friends. In fact, I appreciate how my hands have been there for me as I cook and bake. They allow me to share love by guiding me in the preparation. What a blessing!

They were there for me to hold my son, my grandchildren and my great-grandson and to wipe away their tears. Showing motherly love through the touch.

My hands are my support, always by my side to lend help to those in need, but most of all to share love with family and friends. But I am reminded they are my windows to the world, a constant companion. Because we need both, it matters not if you are left- or right-handed.

So, thank you, hands and an extra thanks to my left hand for not letting the slights hold me back!!

Adinkra Symbols

Adinkrahene	Greatness
Akoben	Call to Action
Ankh	Life
Dwennimmen	Strength & Humility
Fie Hankare	Safety & Security
Gye Nyame	Omnipotence of God
Nsoroma	Faith
Nyame Biribi Wo Soro	Hope
Nyame Dura	Presence of God
Odo Nyera Fie Kwan	Love, Faith & Devotion
Sankofa	Learn from the Past